Praise for

Beginning Seed Saving for the Home Gardener

My garden checklist hasn't included "save seeds!" for way too long. Why? I was waiting for someone to tackle the how and why of it in a way that made sense to me. For the first time in 30+ years, I'm finally ready to take gardening to a whole new level. Independence, here I come, James Ulager by my side.

—MaryJane Butters, Idaho farmer, author, and editor of
MaryJanesFarm magazine, now in its 19th year, and author, *Wild Bread*

Beginning Seed Saving for the Home Gardener is a comprehensive guide to learn how to begin seed saving, or take it to the next level. Yet the book is written in a friendly style, as if the author is speaking to you as a friend. His humorous way of giving information makes it easier to understand.

—Judy Newman, Administrator, Seeds of Diversity

After years of watching Jim Ulager inspire and inform crowds of beginning seed savers at the Common Ground Fair, I'm delighted to see him put it into a book. Not that there aren't already a number of sources available, but this one stands out as accessible and de-mystifying. His target audience is the gardener and would-be seed saver who wishes to take it to the next level, but who may be daunted by the technical jargon of professionals. Ulager brings it down to the basics, with enough botanical detail to explain what you're doing without discouraging you. While the experts may say: if you can't do it this way, then don't even bother, Ulager says: go ahead and take back our ownership of the seed.

—Will Bonsall, director, Scatterseed Project

This engagingly written book contains everything you need to know to save your own garden seeds. The author's goal was to put seed saving back in the hands of home gardeners and he has most certainly accomplished that! His clear explanations and wealth of practical tips de-mystify seed saving and make this an excellent resource for novices and experienced seed savers alike.

—Linda Gilkeson, author, *Backyard Bounty 2nd edition* and *The Complete Guide to Year-Round Organic Gardening in the Pacific Northwest*

This book is a great introduction for those new to seed saving and is a good companion to *Seed Libraries*. It encourages you to be observant in your garden and to learn from your plants.

—Cindy Conner, Homeplace Earth, and author, *Seed Libraries* and *Grow a Sustainable Diet*

beginning
SEED
saving

for the **home gardener**

Jim Ulager

new society
PUBLISHERS

Cover design by Diane McIntosh.
Cover Images © iStock
Interior Photographs © James Ulager 2019, unless otherwise noted.

Printed in Canada. First printing September 2019.

Inquiries regarding requests to reprint all or part of *Beginning Seed Saving for the Home Gardener* should be addressed to New Society Publishers at the address below. To order directly from the publishers, please call toll-free (North America) 1-800-567-6772, or order online at www.newsociety.com

Any other inquiries can be directed by mail to:
New Society Publishers
P.O. Box 189, Gabriola Island, BC V0R 1X0, Canada
(250) 247-9737

LIBRARY AND ARCHIVES CANADA CATALOGUING IN PUBLICATION

Title: Beginning seed saving for the home gardener / Jim Ulager.
Names: Ulager, Jim, 1977– author.
Description: Includes index.
Identifiers: Canadiana (print) 20190139692 | Canadiana (ebook) 20190139706 |
ISBN 9780865719262 (softcover) | ISBN 9781550927191 (PDF) |
ISBN 9781771423151 (EPUB)
Subjects: LCSH: Vegetables—Seeds. | LCSH: Vegetables—Seeds—Harvesting. |
LCSH: Vegetables—Propagation. | LCSH: Vegetables—Reproduction. |
LCSH: Vegetable gardening.
Classification: LCC SB324.75 .U43 2019 | DDC 635—dc23

Funded by the Government of Canada — Financé par le gouvernement du Canada

New Society Publishers' mission is to publish books that contribute in fundamental ways to building an ecologically sustainable and just society, and to do so with the least possible impact on the environment, in a manner that models this vision.

Contents

Acknowledgments vii

Part I: Seed Saving Belongs in the Home Garden 1

  A. Where Have All the Seed-Savers Gone? 1

  B. How This Book is Different 3

  C. How to Read This Book 3

  D. Why Should We Save Seed 4

Part II: Saving Seed: What We Need to Know About Our
Plants in Order to Save Seed—General Principles 11

  A. How Exciting Do You Like It?
Vegetative vs. Sexual Propagation 11

  B. You Look So Much Like Your Mother!
Is My Plant a Hybrid or Open-Pollinated? 17

  C. How Plants Do It, Part I: Plant Sexual Anatomy 20

  D. How Plants Do It, Part II:
How Do They Get Together? 20

  E. How Deep is Your Gene Pool?
Inbreeding vs. Outbreeding 24

  F. Promiscuity vs. Prudence. How to Improve the Odds
You Will Get the Result You Are Looking For
(or Something Better!) 25

Part III: If It's Your First Time: Easy Inbreeding Plants
with Perfect Flowers 31

  A. Peas and Beans 31

  B. Lettuce 33

  C. Tomatoes 35

  D. Peppers 38

Part IV: Plants with Moving Parts 39
  A. The Squash Family 39
  B. Spinach 44
  C. Easy(er) Biennials 45

Part V: Not as Hard as They Look—Biennials and
  Obligate Outbreeders 53
  A. Corn 53
  B. Carrots and Parsnip 56
  C. The Cabbage Family 58

Part VI: What Have We Missed? 63
  A. Cucumbers 63
  B. Melons 64
  C. Sunflowers 64

Part VIII: Strategies for Success 67
  A. Curing Seed, Seed Storage, and Longevity 67
  B. Biennials and Winter Storage 70
  C. Threshing and Winnowing 72
  D. Space-Saving Strategies 76
  E. A Drying House 77

Part VII: Final Recommendations: Try It! 81

  Index 83
  About the Author 87
  About New Society Publishers 88

Acknowledgments

As I consider the many people who in some way touched not only the creation of this book—but also the Vermont garden that inspired it— I feel blessed to recognize the many people who have touched the lives of our family. I am grateful for my father, whose stories of a 1930 coal miner's subsistence garden started me on the path. (If you had known the effect it would have, would you have dared to share with me?) For my mother, who taught me to cook—the other inspiration for my garden! For my mother-in-law, Cindy, whose gentle appreciation for the natural world convinced me that "ornamentals are plants, too", and for sharing her peaceful garden, which kept me going during the short years I lived in the city. For Will Bonsall, who not only shared his deep well of seed-saving and homesteading, but who showed unending patience and encouragement for a novice. (The sections on openness and experimentation would never have come to life without you, Will!). For Ingrid Witvoet, for seeing something worthwhile in my homespun musings at the Common Ground Fair. For the whole team at New Society Publishers, for your patience with the timeline of a working father of three (and one more to come!). For my children, Anna, Abigail, Joseph, and (the one we will soon meet!) who love dirt under their fingernails. (Just scrub them before we visit Grandma's!)

And most of all, I am grateful for my dear wife, Alicia. For your patience with my gardening habit. For always smiling when you say, "What outbuilding are you building now?" For your encouragement at every potato, onion, pepper, and bean (however glorious or meager). And for your loving partnership in creating the family life captured in these pages.

PART I

Seed Saving Belongs in the Home Garden

A. Where Have All the Seed-Savers Gone?

One of the most delightful aspects of gardening in northern New England—so much so that it almost makes up for the climate—is the great multitude of amazing gardeners one gets to meet and, more importantly, learn from. Experts abound at the seed store, the community garden, and the farmers' market, on public radio, and for that matter, at the post office, the gas station, and the workplace. No matter where you are, if you have a gardening question, chances are there is someone who can help nearby. And so, when my wife Alicia and I finally had the fortune to have a piece of ground to call our own, we got plenty of direction on how to make and apply compost, how to keep the critters at bay, and the preferred method of canning tomatoes (the freezer is the only way!). There was no shortage of good advice from myriad gardeners that seemed to be able to produce just about anything from our cool, stony soil—except for one glaring exception. Even as the offspring of last year's sunflowers seeds, fallen to the ground and missed by careless squirrels, surrounded the community garden in town, and tomatoes and squash sprang from every compost pile, all of the seed came from the catalogue or the corner store. People who would defiantly (and admirably!) refuse to eat a tomato not grown by themselves or a local farmer, routinely obtained their seed commercially, sometimes from thousands of miles away. Why?

The reason became blindingly clear to me one afternoon when I was attending an agricultural conference and I had the opportunity to hear experts from an agricultural extension (not from my home state of Vermont) give a talk on seed saving. The talk was excellent as they discussed the proper ways to save seed from some of the simplest plants: beans, peas, and tomatoes. As they moved on to discuss other vegetables, however, I heard a phrase that explained my entire experience with seed saving thus far. I remember it something like this: "For a lot of vegetables, if you can't save seed from at least two hundred plants in your home garden, don't even bother. Just buy them from a professional." This advice to a room of folks who included homesteaders who not only grew a lot of their own food but built their own homes, cut their own firewood, and even spun their own yarn. Seeds, though, that should be left to the professionals. From this point on, I vowed to push the limits of seed saving in my own garden.

Now, a word in defense of these highly competent agriculture extension agents: they are not incorrect. Many of our favorite garden crops—cabbages, carrots, onions, leeks, and, most notoriously, corn— do much, much better in larger populations. This truth, however, is incomplete. The conclusion that we should abandon seed saving to professionals is, therefore, flawed. It assumes the goal of the home garden seed saver is exactly the same as it is for commercial grows: maximum uniformity, scale, and consistency. While we can empathize with at least some of these goals, they do not always resonate most with the home gardener. Consider the frugal homesteader who finds a hundred-dollar annual seed purchase unaffordable. What of the gardener who finds an unknown (but delicious!) tomato growing in the compost pile and wants to try to propagate it? What of the woman who grew up eating her Polish grandmother's homemade sauerkraut and receives as her inheritance a single envelope of seed marked simply "cabbage"? Should she simply grow these seeds out while they last, enjoying her grandmother's heirloom for a season (or two or three), and then move on to growing whatever seed is being commercially mass-produced and marketed at the corner store? Is that what she is going to leave *her* grandchildren?

If I make no other case in this book, I would like to leave you with this: seed saving does *not* belong to a small group of experts. It is not the exclusive right of professional large-scale farms. Most of all, it is not to be delegated to industry. It is *ours*. Yours and mine. It is ours by inheritance from our agrarian ancestors, who did it by necessity and—I like to think—out of love for what they were passing along to future generations. To *us*. I propose that now, by a different necessity—and with no less love for our children who follow us—we take it back!

KEEPING IT SIMPLE

We often let ourselves be convinced that seed saving is too hard to do at home. This is untrue. Seed saving belongs in the home garden.

B. How this Book is Different

There are a number of good books on seed saving. I would not have committed the time to writing another one unless I felt sure that there was a piece missing, and that is this: a book about seed saving in the home garden—with all of its trials and difficulties—written by someone who does just that—seed saving in the home garden. While I will discuss techniques used by commercial growers, like separating various seeds by quarter of a mile or more, I will not dwell on these, and will offer alternatives to techniques that seem impractical (at best) for application in the home garden.

C. How to Read This Book

I have set out to provide all the information you need to be successful at seed saving, while avoiding the temptation to provide so much information as to be overwhelming. I fully anticipate that some folks will want more detail in one section and less in others. To balance these needs, look for the "Keeping it Simple" summaries at the end of each section (except the shorter sections that are already pretty well simplified). If you find yourself getting cross-eyed (or impatient with my rambling), just jump to the summary. While there is a lot to say about seed saving, in the end it's just taking

KEEPING IT SIMPLE

If the text seems complicated, see the "Keeping it Simple" summary. Or better yet, just put the book down, go out into your garden, plant some seed you saved, and learn from what happens!

a seed from your garden and keeping it safe and dry until it's time to plant. Let's try not to make it much more complicated than that!

D. Why Should We Save Seed

Before we jump in to *how* to save seed, it is worth noting *why* we should save seed. Not only will this keep us inspired, it will influence some of our techniques.

The Seeds are There

While I have precious few mountain-climbing analogies to apply to seed saving, George Mallory's famous quote that he climbed Everest "because it was there" is a good one.

Have you ever grown black or pinto beans? Well, there are your seeds. Likewise, do you routinely pick *all* of your green beans so that none of them go by and get tough (yeah, right!)? There are always a few at the end. Let them firm up a bit and, *voila!*, there are your green bean seeds for next year.

My favorite example of this was the time I had a half a dozen kale plants live through the winter. I had a lot to do that spring, and by the time I got to that corner of the garden, they had flowered. I let them go. Do you know how many seeds six kale plants can produce? I had a mason jar's full of seed—enough for the county, I joked to myself (and given how hot Vermonters are on their kale, that is saying something!).

After my experience of accidentally saving kale seed, I did three things that transformed my seed saving practice:

1. I marveled at how much Mother Nature was willing to give me freely if I just gave her some room to work;
2. I gave kale seed to anyone who wanted it;
3. I didn't buy that variety of kale seed myself for several years (if I'd had the foresight to put some in the freezer, I'm not sure I'd ever have to buy kale seed again).

After seven or eight years, I dumped what was left of the seed in with the feed grain of some pigs we were growing through the winter. Now,

I thought that seed was too old to germinate, but given the amount of kale growing next spring all over the pig run (and not just near the trough) it apparently had plenty of life left in it. (Either than or the journey through the pig's belly woke it right up!)

If you have strong feelings about exactly *what* these seeds turn into (and in most cases you will!) there is some nuance to understand. We'll get to that. For now I make one humble suggestion: the next time your garden freely gives you seed, plant it and see what happens! Sometimes it will be exactly what you expect and want. Sometimes it won't. The latter is the best teacher.

Frugality

Why do you have a vegetable garden? So many reasons! Fresh food? Yep. To stay busy? Um, maybe once I'm retired, but with three kids I'm already good on that one. To decrease your carbon footprint? Sure! For fun? Well, yes, most of the time. While some are happy to spend more on their garden than the

Another reason to save seeds is seeing your plants all grown up. We usually eat zucchinis when they are 7 or 8 inches long. They need to be fully grown, however, in order to contain ripe seed. One caution, however, is that if you don't keep an eye on them, they may be turned into baby dolls. I found this one tucked in for the night in our daughter's toy cradle.

sum of its economic output, for others of us gardening might be the most economical way to put fresh food on the table. Whichever situation you are in, saving some seed will make a big impact on the economy of your gardening. Consider my kale example from above. While I couldn't use all of it, imagine how much it would have cost me to buy peanut butter jars full of kale seed! (My only regret is that I did not use some for sprouting greens!)

Broader Horizons

The *Garden Seed Inventory* published by the Seed Savers Exchange aims to catalogue all of the commercially available vegetable garden seeds available for sale in the United States and Canada. In 2005, they listed nearly 8500 different unique non-hybrid varieties. That accounts for all of the different tomatoes, green beans, peppers, salad greens, sweet corn—whatever you might grow in your garden, there are about 8500 choices all in.

The Seed Saver Exchange also publishes a yearbook of seeds offered by its members. These are not commercial growers selling their seed, but home gardeners willing to send you some of the seed they grown in their own gardens if you give them a little donation to cover postage and hassle. There are nearly 14,000 unique varieties offered by Seed Saver Exchange members– almost twice as many as you can buy commercially. The thing is, these are not people *selling* their seed—they are gardeners *sharing* seed. The idea is that you will be saving them yourself and, ideally, reoffering them back to the community as a member of the exchange. The punchline: you'll have access to a much greater variety of vegetables if you are willing to put in the effort of saving them yourself.

The opportunities go beyond formal exchanges. Ever go to the farmers' market and bring home the best tomato ever? Save some seeds, grow it out, and see what happens! (See Tomato section for more info on *what* might happen!) My brother-in-law's father got some of the best tomatoes for a northern climate that I had ever tasted. "What variety are they," I asked. His answer socked me: "No idea. Got 'em from a guy from Russia who used to live down the street. Now I grow them and save the seed myself." He gave me a few seeds, and they have been a mainstay of our summer diet ever since.

Sadly, my brother-in-law lost his father a few years ago now. While this was a sad time, it is difficult to

KEEPING IT SIMPLE

Why we choose to save seed will inform to some degree *how* we save seed. More on this later.

There are several reasons to save seed including saving money, having access to more varieties of seeds than those commercially available, and the opportunity to select seeds to do better in our garden year over year.

describe the effect of seeing his tomatoes sprout anew each spring and fill our plates with that familiar acidic sweetness. I say this in no casual way: this is food for the soul. What a loss if we had not been able to save those seeds, not only for ourselves and our garden, but possibly for the plant. I have no idea who else—if anyone—is saving those Russian tomatoes (which I now call "Zurovchak" after the man who supplied them to me).

The important point here is this: if we leave seed saving completely to industry, who will save seeds like the Zurovchak tomato? And if we lose varieties like that, what will happen to the diversity of genetics available to plant breeders as we encounter new pressures on our garden such as diseases and climate change? Our conclusion: seed saving belongs in the home garden!

Evolving With Your Garden

This is perhaps my favorite reason to save seed, but it's a bit complicated. The following story explains it best.

When we first began gardening, we wanted to grow dry beans for chili and baked beans. We didn't have much space, so we wanted pole beans for better yield, and I was enticed by the description of "True

---

Selection

When you have a group of plants (in my example above, dry beans), and you save *only* the seed of plants with certain characteristics (in this case, early maturity), you are practicing *selection*. Technically, you no longer have the exact same variety. That said, this is a perfectly legitimate activity. Just be sure that if you share the seed, you let people know what you're up to. If I were to reoffer my True Red Cranberry Pole bean at a seed saving society, I would have to call it, "Jim's Early Selection of Cranberry Pole" or something like that. As you are (hopefully) starting to notice, I strongly encourage folks to consider their gardens as ongoing experiments. When you share your results, however, just be clear with people about what you are giving them!

Red Cranberry Pole Bean" in a seed catalogue. Not only did they look unique, but they were a Native American variety from central Maine—how cool! The first year I grew them out in our northern Vermont climate, however, I was befuddled that they came from central Maine. They barely ripened before a hard killing frost had its way with our garden in the early fall, and they had to survive some pretty close calls with light frost to get even that far. It was during one of these close calls that I decided to save just a few beans as seed from those plants that were ripening first. Doing this guaranteed a seed crop, though we were fortunate enough to get good food crops as well.

About Experimentation

The best advice I can give you about selection—or anything else in seed saving for that matter—is to experiment. I have learned so much from doing things I have been told not to do (I'm talking strictly seed saving here, of course, right!), even though sometimes the results have been downright disastrous. Once I wanted to try saving leek seed. We loved eating leeks but didn't have much space for them. Unlike some vegetables, you can't eat your leeks and save them for seed, too. So, what to do? I simply took the biggest, most succulent-looking leeks and put them on the table with some butter and potatoes. I took the wimpiest, smallest ones that would have not added much to the table, and what,

in my great wisdom, did I do with those? You guessed it: that was my seed stock. I hope you can see where this is heading because, at the time, I did not. I planted those leeks out the next year to grow to seed (see Biennials). I was so proud when they sprouted nice round flower heads. I immediately showed my wife the beautiful viable seed I got, and lots of it. I planted that seed the next year and…

Let's just say the apple (or in this case—the leek) doesn't fall far from the tree. We had skinny, wimpy-looking leeks that were "just like mom and dad." While I didn't plant any more of that leek seed, it was one of the most valuable seed crops I've ever grown (metaphorically speaking, of course).

I hope that from whatever comfy place you are reading this book, you might be able to anticipate what would happen if you took the earliest maturing plants as seed and replanted it year over year. I'm not too proud to admit it: I had no idea what I was doing, though it has a name. It's called selection. I was selecting for those plants that matured earliest, and indeed, pretty soon I was astounded to see that the plants began to mature earlier and earlier and were no longer threatened by frost every fall. What a remarkable thing I did to improve my garden, without really knowing what I was up to! If you'd have asked me then how best to improve your garden, I might say with more compost, good crop rotation, etc., etc. Who knew that helping your seeds along by teaching them what it is you value most out of them was something a humble home gardener could do? This shouldn't surprise us, however. Again, our ancestors have done this for millennia.

When you are open to seeing your garden as an experiment, you don't always get the results you expect, but often you do get lucky and learn something new!

This is absolutely my favorite reason to save seed: we grow together. Every year they teach me something, and I teach them in return. With good stewardship, the soil not only gets a little richer, but my plants get to know it a little better. The garden is not *my* sole endeavor, then, but a collaboration. The plants, the seeds, the soil, and the gardener—we all grow together.

PART II

Saving Seed

What We Need to Know About Our Plants in Order to Save Seed—General Principles

Now that we've waved the banner of *why* we save seed, let's get to the fun part and talk about *how* we save seed. These two questions, the "how" and the "why," aren't unrelated, as we will see.

In this section, we'll be setting the stage for how we can approach seed saving for most any garden plant, asking seven simple questions:

1. Does this plant reproduce by *sexual* or *vegetative propagation*?
2. Is the variety you would like to propagate a *hybrid* or *open-pollinated*?
3. Is this an *annual* (bearing seed in the first year) or *biennial* (bearing in the second year)?
4. *Where* are the plant's *male* and *female* parts?
5. Is this an *outbreeding* or *inbreeding* plant?
6. How does do those parts (or genetic material from those parts) get together—known as *pollination*?
7. Are there any factors that might influence the *purity* of our seed?

A. How Exciting Do You Like It?
Vegetative vs. Sexual Propagation

OK. Let's get it right out there. For the most part, when we are talking about seed saving, we will be discussing plant sex. There is one notable exception, however, and those are plants that reproduce by vegetative propagation. There is no true seed formed, and no exchange of genetic material. In other words, no sex.

Vegetative Propagation

Before you get too concerned for these poor plants that appear to have been committed to life of celibacy by mere circumstance, most of them are actually quite capable of reproducing sexually. However, for various reasons, generations of gardeners have found it more convenient to reproduce them without all the complications of sex. (Who knew that it was complicated for plants, too?) Because we're going to discuss sexual propagation for most of the rest of the book, I'm going to dwell here on a few garden vegetables (and some fruits) that are typically reproduced vegetatively.

1. Apples, pears, and several fruit trees

I start with fruit trees as they are possibly the easiest example to understand, but one that is commonly misunderstood. We all know apples have seeds, right? And apple trees have flowers. (For the rest of this

Strawberries are another plant typically reproduced vegetatively. The runner pictured here will soon root and become a new strawberry plant, an exact genetic copy of its parent.

book, when you hear 'flower" think plant sex part.) So, why are apples in the vegetative propagation section?

The answer is this: if you want an apple tree that is *true to type*, that is, produces the same kinds of apples as its parent tree (let's say, in this case, a Macintosh), you take a small cutting from a branch of that tree and graft it onto whatever root you want to use for your new tree. This way, the fruit-bearing wood has the same genetics as its parent (in this case, Macintosh genetics). If instead you plant the seeds from that Macintosh apple, you will get different genetics: half of the genes from the mother apple tree, the other half from whatever other tree (typically not the Macintosh tree itself—to be discussed later, in the Sexual Propagation section) that provided the pollen to that flower.

To that end, you might want a tree with slightly different characteristics than the parent. If you want to develop a new type of apple tree with, say, the taste of a Macintosh and the storage ability of a Keepsake, you can save the seed of a Mac-pollinated by Keepsake. You might get a keeper that tastes like Mac. Pears and many other fruit trees work the same way.

2. Potatoes

Like apples, if you want potatoes with the same characteristics as their parent plant, then you plant a part of that plant (in this case, the tuberous root) instead of the true seed. That said, potatoes have all the moving parts necessary to make flowers and therefore, true seed. As with the apple example, this is how we get new potato varieties. Pollen from potato variety A (say, Yukon Gold) lands on a flower from another variety (say, Kennebec). The small tomato-like fruits will produce seed. The result from this cross may be something very good, perhaps with the taste of Yukon Gold and the productivity of Kennebec. I say *may* because every pollination event will be different. Just like with humans, two parents who have several children produce siblings, not identical twins—you could get a number of different types of potato varieties from that Yukon/Kennebec cross.

If this is a bit confusing, here is the bottom line for all of us except potato breeders: if you want Kennebec potatoes, you don't plant the seed, you plant the potato. This is how you get the same genetics (that is, plant characteristics) year after year.

3. Other Plants That We Save by Vegetative Propagation

a) Garlic—Cloves are harvested in the summer, divided, and planted in the fall to produce bulbs the next summer.

b) Sweet potatoes—Vines grow from the tubers in warm, moist conditions, and then are picked and planted out to form the new plants.

c) Jerusalem artichokes—Native to the Northeast US, these tubers divide so aggressively that this is a plant that is difficult *not* to have come back every year. (Full of dietary fiber, try some in place of potatoes in your favorite recipe, or just roast them up. So delicious, so healthy!)

d) Woody herbs—While also grown from seed, herbs like rosemary can be grown from cuttings. I find it works best in the spring, but I've had success throughout the year. Snip the last three inches off a vigorous branch—pull the leaves off the bottom inch or so. Plant in a small block of moist soil in a warm, well-lit area but out of direct sunlight at first. Rooting hormone will increase percentage of success, but is not necessary—just plant a few extra to make up for failed cuttings. Cover with a mason jar to prevent moisture loss for 2–3 weeks while the plants set roots, and the plants will set roots.

Pick garlic when the bottom two or three leaves are dried down and the rest is still green. Hang in a dry, shady spot until early fall to cure for storage. Store in a cool, dry place.

Benefits and Challenges of Vegetative Propagation

Because one of the primary challenges of producing true seed (sexual reproduction) is purity, vegetative propagation tends to be a little easier. The genetics of the child are going to be exactly the same as the genetics of the parent. That said, it also presents a few specific challenges:

1. **Disease.** This is the primary challenge with vegetative propagation. Potatoes are a great example. The Irish potato famine was the result of a fungal disease (late blight) that overwinters on live potatoes and infects the next year's crop. Potatoes also can collect viruses that, over time, can diminish plant vigor and productivity.

2. **Grafting.** This isn't so much a problem as an opportunity. Grafting *scion wood* (the branch of a fruit tree) onto a specific root stock allows us to choose things like winter hardiness, precociousness, and tree growing habit (dwarf vs full-size)—all attributes affected by the root—and still have the type of fruit we want. I include it as a challenge only because it is a skill one must acquire.

The curly 'scape' of this hard-neck garlic will ultimately produce flower capable of sexual reproduction. It is much more efficient, however, to get nice big heads by employing vegetative propagation and using the bulbs from the ground.

3. **Storage**. After disease, this is the other big challenge associated with vegetative propagation, and least in climates with a winter. You can't plant potatoes if they don't make it through the winter. Like grafting, however, this can be an opportunity. For example, the most disease-laden potatoes will spoil in storage (though sadly that is no guarantee when it comes to late blight). This is less of an issue for

KEEPING IT SIMPLE

1. There is no exchange of genetic material (that is, sex) in vegetative propagation.
2. Rather than using seed, material from the body of the plant (such as stems or roots) is used to make new plants in vegetative propagation.
3. The offspring are genetically identical to the parents.
4. The primary challenges can include getting through the winter and propagation of disease.
5. Sexual propagation involves the transfer of genetic material in a flower to produce true seed.

garlic, as it is planted in the fall (though I've seen over-hungry rodents do some damage to garlic overwintering in the ground, even if it isn't their favorite choice). For a more detailed discussion on storage issues, see the section on Biennials.

Sexual Propagation

We defined vegetative propagation as the creation of new plants without the exchange of genetic material. Logically, then, sexual propagation involves that exchange. This can get a bit confusing, as some plants can exchange that material with themselves. "What" you say? "Plant sex doesn't necessarily take two individuals?" Well, no, in fact it doesn't. And sometimes it requires many, many more than that. *Don't* blush here, but *do* see the sections on How Plants Do It and Inbreeding vs. Outbreeding for more details. Another way to think sexual propagation is that it involves the production of seed from a flower. Some flowers (tomatoes) are a bit more obvious than others (corn), but flowers just the same. And while catalogues sell "seed potatoes" and "seed garlic," don't confuse these with true seed. These were reproduced vegetatively. The term "seed" here simply means that they have been certified disease-free and suitable for planting.

If you know how people make babies, it's not that hard to learn how plants make seeds. And the results can be just as adorable.

B. You Look So Much Like Your Mother: Is My Plant a Hybrid or Open-Pollinated?

One of the first things you want to know before you save a vegetable for seed is whether the *variety* you have chosen is *open-pollinated* or a *hybrid*. There are a few important terms there so let's dwell on them for just a moment.

A *variety* is the particular version of the vegetable you are growing. For example, if you're growing tomatoes, the varieties might include Brandywine, Sungold, or Purple Cherokee. In this example, Brandywine and Cherokee are open-pollinated varieties whereas Sungold is a hybrid variety.

Now that we understand what we mean by variety, the easiest way to understand open-pollinated versus hybrid is to consider the relationship between the plant you are growing, its parents, and its prospective children. Let's continue with the example of tomatoes. Brandywine is an open-pollinated variety. That means its parents were Brandywine tomatoes, it's grandparents were Brandywine tomatoes, and if we do everything correctly, its children will also be Brandywine tomatoes. Hybrid varieties are different. Sungold's parents are not Sungold tomatoes. Likewise, if you save Sungold tomato seeds and grow them out, you will not get Sungold tomatoes, but you will get an interesting assortment of characteristics of Sungold. Most of the plants might bear small fruit but some will bear large fruit. Likewise, some plants will bear yellow or orange fruit, but others might bear red fruit. For this reason, for most of us, most of the time, we are going to want to make sure we are saving seeds from open-pollinated varieties.

Now it is possible in some cases to stabilize an open-pollinated variety out of hybrid offspring. Clear Dawn is a lovely open-pollinated onion that was grown as a stabilized stock out of the hybrid onion Copra. Here, *stabilization* simply refers to the fact that the offspring are for the most part predictable and uniform. It turns out this is much easier to do in some cases than others (does not work well for Sungolds, for example). Any detailed explanation of the process is well beyond our scope here.

One other term you may see paired with the word hybrid is *F1*, or *F1 hybrid*. This stands for *first filial*, or the first offspring from a cross. For our purposes, when you see F1, it's typically being used as a shorthand to denote that a particular variety is a hybrid.

Going forward, we are going to focus on techniques for saving open-pollinated seed. In discussing each different plant, I will point out how likely you are to find open-pollinated varieties vs. hybrids. Modern sweet corn, for example, is almost exclusively available as hybrid varieties, though some old-fashioned (and by some still very well-loved) varieties of open-pollinated sweet corn can be found. Dry beans, on the other hand, are a different matter. There are oodles and oodles of open-pollinated options.

This brings us to our last question on the matter: what if you don't know if you have an open-pollinated or hybrid variety? Start by considering the source of the seed. Many seed companies and catalogues make it clear in their catalogue or website, or right on the packaging. A few, however, do not. As a backup, you may be able to find the same variety listed in another catalogue. Seeds you get from friends or neighbors that they have saved over the years are going to be open-pollinated, though it's never a bad idea to ask. "Hey, these seeds look really cool. Did you grow them out yourself?" This is not only a nice way of showing your admiration for their seed-saving skills, but also a subtle way of making sure they didn't come right out of a seed packet or another source. Of course, in the end, there may be no way to know for sure if you have an open-pollinated variety or not. In that case— well, I hope you know by now what I'm going to recommend. That's right! Plant it and see what happens!

KEEPING IT SIMPLE

Before saving a plant for seed, check to see if the variety you have is open-pollinated (meaning the parents and potential offspring are likely to all have similar characteristics) or an F1 hybrid (meaning a cross between two different parents, in which case the outcome of the seed will be somewhat unpredictable).

KEEPING IT SIMPLE

It's totally OK to experiment with the offspring of hybrid plants, just be open to what you might get. Beware of laws regarding patented varieties.

My Mother-in-Law's Experience
With a Hardy Hybrid Volunteer Tomato

One common circumstance when you might see what comes of seeds saved from hybrids is with a *volunteer*. This is simply a plant that you did not plant, but sprung up randomly in your garden or compost pile from dropped seeds. Squash, tomatoes, and sunflowers are some common plants that often volunteer themselves. In our northern Vermont climate, tomato volunteers typically emerge much too late in the season to be of much use. However, one year my mother-in-law (who lives in balmy Philadelphia) had the most fantastic volunteer tomatoes in her garden. We were so excited about them; they were substantially lusher, greener, and more robust than every other tomato plant in her garden. This was of particular excitement because her garden is a little shady, and we are wondering if we had hit the jackpot on a shade-tolerant tomato plant.

As the fruit started to emerge, we realized that it didn't look like any of the tomatoes she had planted previously.

We hypothesized that it was a volunteer from a hybrid variety and therefore we were getting, perhaps, to see some of its previously latent traits. We cheered that tomato on all summer and could not wait to taste it. She called me sometime in late July. Robust and hardy as that tomato plant looked, its fruit tasted just awful. Watery and insipid, blech! Bummer. A wasted experiment? Well, no, I would argue. If you do that a dozen or more times, eventually you are going to come across a real winner. Similarly, if we were interested in crossing that tomato with one with better flavor, we might be able to coax out a sweet, hardy, delicious, shade-loving tomato. This time, though, the plant just went into the compost. We had lots of other gardening to do!

You should definitely experiment, but that doesn't make you duty-bound to find a good practical use out of every experiment. The most succulent fruit of every experiment is experience.

C. How Plants Do It, Part I: Plant Sexual Anatomy

As you can already tell, I tend to explain plant reproduction in terms of human sexuality. As Will Bonsall, Director of the Scatterseed Project, puts it, "We all know how we do it." (Footnote: What do you do if you don't know how we do it? When I'm speaking to a group, I typically offer to discuss matter with anyone who requires further explanation after the talk. Surprisingly, no one has ever taken me up on this. For logistical reasons, please forgive me if I refer you, my dear reader, to your mom, dad, or responsible older sibling.) I have spoken with Will on beginning and advanced seed saving (respectively) for many years now, and we habitually use words like "male and female" or "boy and girl" parts instead of "anther" or "pistil" or "stamen," and for clarity's sake, I will do so here.

So yes, plants that reproduce sexually have male parts that produce pollen (the equivalent of sperm) and a female part that bears the seed or fruit (the equivalent of a placenta for the germ within the seed that will become the new seedling). What keeps us on our toes is exactly where these parts are!

1. Some plants have *perfect flowers*. These are flowers with male and female parts on the same flower. This is relatively common: peas, beans, tomatoes, peppers, cabbage family, fruit trees, to name a few.
2. Some plants have male and female parts on different flowers. Squash is a classic example here. The female flower is distinguishable by the mini (yet unpollinated) fruit at its base. Corn is another example. The pollen is produced at top of the stalk, while each kernel on the cob is a small ovum.
3. In some cases, the male and female parts are actually on different plants. To that end, there are male and female individuals, just like people. This is the case with spinach, though you'd never know unless you let the poor things grow up long enough to see adolescence!

D. How Plants Do It, Part II: How do they get together?

I remember in fifth grade going on a field trip to our local science center. On the permission slip, our parents had to give permission not only to go, but to attend a special session where a well-qualified teacher would explain to us the "Wonder of Wonders." While this was code language to my pre-adolescent mind, the teacher made it quite clear when the session started that we were going to learn how babies were made. She went into very explicit detail about how our bodies are when we're small, and how they change as we grow into men and women. We discussed how men have sperm and women have eggs, and that it was in the getting together of the egg and the sperm that a baby was made. I recall my oh-so-courageous friend raising his hand and tentatively asking the question we were all just dying to know: "Yes, but, um, just how do they get together?" The reply came swiftly: "Just a moment, dear." We went on to discuss that, after fertilization, there is an embryo that implants itself in the uterus and forms a placenta—among other things. On and on, development and growth and kicking, and finally, *voilà!* Nine months later a baby is born. Looking back as an adult, it feels like the nine-month wait for each of my three children didn't last half as long as that class. Somewhere in there, she did in fact explain how the sperm got from the man into the woman. She didn't call it sex, though, and whatever she called it, it left us with a lot more questions than answers. And much speculation on the bus ride back home.

What does this tale have to teach us about seed saving? Our fifth-grade minds were befuddled by biology, so much so as to miss the practical aspects of the subject (and perhaps at this tender point in our life, not without good reason). We shall make no such mistake here, however. So, that leads to the same question my brave classmate asked all those years ago—or, at least, a similar question. "Um, so just how do plants do it?"

Plant sex, or to use the more proper term, pollination, can occur in one of three ways:

1. **Self Pollination:** In most cases, self-pollination is the most hassle-free as it involves the least moving parts. This involves a perfect flower (remember, these have both male and female parts on the same flower) that is receptive to its own pollen. The pollen simply falls from the male part of the flower right onto the female part of the same flower. All done! In many cases, this happens so early that by the time the flower is truly open, the pollination is complete, so

unintended crossing is much less of an issue. If we appreciate the evolutionary benefits of trading genes with other individuals (as we should) we can see why many plants—including many with perfect flowers—have mechanisms in place to make sure they don't accept their own pollen. Those plants that do self-pollinate, however, make prime candidates for seed saving in the home garden. Beans, peas, tomatoes, lettuce, and peppers are all great examples that we will discuss in further detail later.

2. **Insect Pollination:** Perhaps the most common method of pollen transfer, both in the garden and in nature at large, is insect pollination. This involves an insect visiting a male flower (or male flower part) to gather nectar, and bringing grains of pollen along for the ride, until that same insect runs into the female part of a different flower of the same type of plant. Apples, pears, blueberries, squash, the cabbage family (cabbage, kale, broccoli), carrots, parsley, onions, leeks and many, many more vegetables are insect-pollinated.

We have to consider a few things when saving seed for these vegetables. First, do we have an environment that is favorable to pollinators? Perhaps most important is avoiding insecticides. Likewise, having a breadth of flowering plants available throughout the growing season also helps, as the flowers of our food plants typically do not provide enough food for the whole season. Second, when a pollinator is visiting the female parts of our plants, we have to think about where else she may have been. What other male flowers may she have visited? We will discuss this in detail under "Promiscuity versus Prudence."

When considering pollinators, we often think of the honeybee. While she is among the most excellent and most able of all pollinators, we need to keep in mind the numerous other insects involved in pollination—which is among the most important job in all of nature. Dozens of other types of bees, flies, wasps, and mosquitoes do it too—some better for one plant and some better for another. A detailed exploration is, once again, beyond our scope here, but an appreciation for the myriad beneficial pollinators that grace our gardens should not be lost. Happy are they who awake in the morning to hear their gardens buzzing with the diligent activity of hundreds of these welcome creatures.

When you are out in the garden listening to that pollinator buzz, you may notice one inconsistency: those pollinators are visiting my beans, peas, and tomatoes! What's that all about? I thought those were self-pollinators? Well, yes, they are. But they still have pollen, and insects will still go for it. It's just that there is some mechanism that makes it difficult (never impossible) for insects to carry the fertile pollen from one flower and deliver it to the fertile female part of another flower. The nuance of this will become clearer as we consider each vegetable in turn.

3. Wind Pollination: As a devoted father, I have a really difficult time understanding wind pollination. These are plants that simply release millions and millions to tiny pollen grains off into the wind, to find whichever mothers and seek whatever fortune lies ahead. Such is the fate of a wind-pollinated plant. From an evolution standpoint, we can see the benefits: large numbers of plants releasing large amounts of pollen off into the breeze, and may the strongest ones survive. For the home gardener, though, this can be a problem. For this reason, wind-pollinated plants, including corn, beets, and chard (beets and chard are the same thing, by the way, just bred for roots vs. leaves), can be the most challenging for the home gardener.

The first challenge here is the fact that, as illustrated above, wind-pollinated plants tend to do well in large populations. (As you see below, we refer to this as being decidedly *outbreeding*). Can you imagine a situation where only a half a dozen or so individuals send their precious genetic material into the wind? There is little chance at all that the pollen would reach a fertile female flower. On the other hand, acres and acres of corn can do very well like this. During the time of pollination, they are living in a cloud of their own pollen—the female silks having no problem finding the tiny, fertile grains of pollen that are filling the air. I don't grow acres of corn in my home garden, though.

The second challenge is purity. While we'll discuss this more below, how do you know that the pollen that fertilized your corn

KEEPING IT SIMPLE

1. Pollination refers to the act of transferring genetic material (pollen) from a male flower part to a female flower part to produce a seed.
2. This process can happen directly by self-pollination, by insect pollination, or by wind pollination

seed came from the same variety of corn? These grains of pollen have been known to travel a mile or more. What if the popcorn you are saving is pollinated by the dairy farmer's field corn across the road? What's more, what if that field corn is genetically engineered to produce its own insecticide, and therefore is not only patented, but is capable of harming the pollinators you've been so carefully cultivating (see Insect Pollination, above)?

Suffice it to say, wind pollination is tricky in the home garden—but it's not impossible! I will discuss some techniques for addressing these very issues in the section on Corn.

E. How Deep is Your Gene Pool?
Inbreeding vs. Outbreeding

Once again, we all know how it works with people, so let's start this section with another human example.

Imagine a dozen of us got so fed up with the world we moved to an island so remote that we had absolutely no contact with the outside world. (Believe me, I've been tempted!) We grew our gardens in peace, and saved all of our own seed (well, we would have to, right?). Things just couldn't be better. Couples form and have children, and we pass along our seed saving knowhow. That first generation of kids grows up and does great. But what happens to their kids (assuming no one leaves or joins the island)? Within just a few generations, people won't be able to avoid having children with someone who isn't in some way pretty closely related. Soon, some genetic difficulties are going to start to emerge, and the colony will cease to thrive. This is because humans are an *outbreeding* species. We do best with a large gene pool of individuals from which to choose our partners in child bearing. More importantly, we cease to thrive when we have offspring with individuals we are closely related to, especially after several generations.

While some plants are very much like humans in this respect, the

You can see the yellow female part of this pepper flower protruding past the male parts. This one is very likely to cross with its neighbors.

The plant teepee in the center left is actually four lettuce plants gone to seed with their stalks tied together. This prevents tipping, which would ruin seed. These were planted in the early spring. It is now late summer, and the rest of that early lettuce planting has been cleared for the emerging fall lettuce crop.

Who says vegetative propagation is no fun? Potato digging time is a family favorite at our house. These will be cured in a cool, dry, dark place for a few weeks before being put away in the root cellar, where they will last until late spring.

Set onions out early in spring, even if it is going to snow again.

Onions need to dry down in a sunny place before storage. A greenhouse or this south-facing screen porch let the sun in and keep the rain out.

They are hardy and typically sprout before the grass turns green.

These onions are ready for a heavy mulching of dry leaves to retain moisture and suppress weeds.

Flower stalks emerge near the solstice.

Seduce pollinators into your garden with some ornamental flowers.

This pretty sweet onion tastes excellent in the fall, but sprouts in the cellar by early December. If you have a cold winter, storage variety onions are a bit easier to get through the winter to their seed-bearing second year.

Everything you need to process tomato seed.

Slice the tomato and use your finger to pull the pulp and seed into a mason jar. Depending on the type of tomato and how clean your fingers are, you can often eat the tomato as well.

Set the jar uncovered where it won't be disturbed. Our northeast-facing kitchen window provides nice access to indirect daylight.

After three to five days, a film will appear on the surface.

Add some water and stir to break the seeds away from the pulp. Pour the pulp out, keeping the seeds at the botton; add a bit more water, and repeat.

When the water is clear, you are done. Note how the seeds sink to the bottom.

Drain the jar and place the seeds on a plate to dry. Separate the seeds so they don't stick togehter.

Start by identifying a female flower by noting the small fruitlet at the base. This should be bagged the night before it opens to avoid early-morning insect pollination.

For every female flower you wish to pollinate, find two or three male flowers, ideally from a different plant. Note the lack of fruitlet at the base.

Remove the male flower from the plant, and peel off the petals. Note the fine grains of pollen.

Dab the pollen from the male flower liberally on the female flower. Be sure to ensure even pollination, or the fruit will abort.

The pollen grains are clearly visible on this hand-pollinated female flower.

The last step is to bag the pollinated female flower for the rest of the day to avoid insect contamination. You should also label the hand-pollinated fruit, as you will not likely hand pollinate every fruit on the plant, and you want to know which ones are good for seed.

Labeling your plantings well is an important first step, particularly if you are growing more than one variety.

Sometimes you get so much of a certain seed that you won't know what to do with it all. Here, we see an extra abundance of kale seed becoming late winter microgreens.

You don't need a lot of space to save seed, particularly if you are strategic about it. Only a few square feet of this garden will be dedicated purely to seed production. Some seed will also be harvested from space where we are simultaneously producing a food crop (like popcorn and winter squash).

You can see that the inner petals of this pea flower are covering all of the sexual parts, preventing any insect interference. By the time those petals open, pollination will have already occurred.

interesting thing is that many are not. While some plants (most notably corn) need a huge population of individuals to have health offspring, others—the *inbreeding* plants—just need a few. Some plants…OK, close your eyes if you are easily embarrassed…just need themselves.

What does this mean for us? Practically, inbreeding plants are the easiest to save in the home garden because you don't have to have a huge field of them to have healthy babies. A few plants will do just fine. Likewise, many inbreeding plants with *perfect flowers* (remember, those flowers that have both male and female parts) are receptive to their own pollen. Yes—they can get themselves pregnant. To that end, there is typically a lower likelihood of crossing with other varieties of the same plant. This leads us to our next essential question—just how loyal are your plants anyway?

KEEPING IT SIMPLE

Inbreeding plants are more tolerant of small populations than are outbreeding plants. While this makes inbreeders a bit easier to save in the home garden, don't be intimidated by outbreeders.

F. Promiscuity vs. Prudence.
How to Improve the Odds You Will Get the Result You Are Looking For (or Something Better!)

As open as I encourage folks to be about the unexpected joys that arise in their gardening, let's face it: at some point, we want a little predictability that the seeds we are saving are going to grow into what we intend them to be. To do this, we'll want to know the parents. Just like with humans, knowing mom is easy—she is where the seed comes from. Knowing dad, on the other hand, can be tricky. What we're saying is, how do we know if there has been a cross between two different varieties, and what's more, how do we prevent that from happening?

How to know if there has been a cross can be trickier for some plants than for others, particularly if the plants you are saving seed for are pretty similar in characteristics. For more discussion on how to tell if varieties have crossed, see my sidebar The Unintended Cross!

To prevent crossing, there are a few techniques you can use:

1. **Growing cross-resistant vegetables.** This is the easiest way. See the sections on Peas and Beans, Lettuce, and Tomatoes for some discussion on how this works for different plants.

2. **Hand pollination.** OK, so it's bad enough that we're discussing plants having sex, but do we really need to discuss how we can directly participate in the act? This can be a very useful technique in maintaining purity when you have a number of different varieties in close proximity. Because it is of significant use in saving squash seed, we will discuss it in detail in that section.

3. **Separating by space.** This is one of the most common ways of preventing a cross between two varieties, but for those of us with small home gardens, it can be a challenge. The amount of spacing you need to provide depends on three things:

    a. **How easily they cross.** For cross-resistant vegetables like peas and beans, most sources recommend 12–25 yards. I personally grow these right next to each other. Squash need 200–300 yards, and wind-pollinated plants like corn need over a mile.

    b. **How important it is to avoid a cross.** The black beans that I boldly grow right next to cranberry and cannellini beans are very precious to me. That said, if I have a cross (as I have, see The Unintentional Cross), it is by no means a disaster. I have lots of stock from years prior and, in a pinch, I can just buy more. It is a readily available commercial variety. On the other hand, I have grown a tomato called Zurovchak that I got from my brother-in-law's father, who is now deceased, who in turn got it decades ago from his neighbor in another state who got it from Russia. I love this tomato. It is huge yet delicate, and ripens beautifully in our northern climate. If I lost it, I would have absolutely no way to replace it. While I typically grow tomatoes right next to each other without any crossing, this is one I should consider separating from other tomatoes by at least 25 yards, if not more. That said, because I maintain a backup supply from previous years (an insurance policy should there be a cross!), I'm perhaps not as diligent as I should be in this regard.

    c. **What else is in the landscape.** The odds that a pollinator might contaminate one of your pumpkins with pollen from another pumpkin 50 yards away depends in large part on what lies between them. If you have a lot else that is in flower, the insects will have so much to keep them busy between the two pumpkin varieties that there will be less of a chance of cross-pollination than if there was simply a field of close-cut grass. All the more reason to show your love to your pollinators by having a wide variety of flowering plants across the season!

4. **Separating by time.** This method of isolation is little talked about and quite useful for the home gardener. You can separate in two ways: within the year or between years.

   a. **Separating within the year.** The Zurovchak tomato that I discussed above is one of my earliest varieties. To that end, it is usually the first one to flower and set fruit. If I save the seed from that first fruit, it has less of a possibility of crossing than if I saved a later fruit. Similarly, of all of my squashes, zucchini are my first to flower. If I give them a little extra help by starting them a week or two before all of my other squashes inside, I can reliably get a few weeks with no squashes in flower in my garden except zucchini. Similarly, by the end of the season, we're often tired of zucchini, but my pumpkins are still setting fruit. If I pull the zucchini up and use those later pumpkins as my seed stock, I can significantly decrease the chance of crossing. My favorite example of

KEEPING IT SIMPLE

1. Unintended crosses with other plant varities can lead to unpredictable outcomes when saving seed.
2. Strategies to prevent these crosses include:
   a. Saving seed from inbreeding self-pollinators (peas, beans, lettuce, and tomato)
   b. Hand pollination (discussed in detail in section on Squash)
   c. Separation by time or space
   d. Caging
3. Crossing with vegetables grown in your neighbor's garden or farm, as well as potential crosses with wild weeds, is a consideration.
4. This will sound much less complicated as we consider each seed in the next section.

separation by time is field corn and popcorn—which I will discuss in detail in the section on Corn.

b. **Separating between years.** This is a good technique to use in one of two situations: 1) if you have a non-perishable crop that you can grow every other year, and 2) biennials. The case for biennials is easy. I can grow five different carrots for a food crop, but because they seed in their second year, as long as I'm only growing one seed crop per year, I don't have to worry about crossing. And, because the carrots will give me tons and tons of seed, I'll have plenty to last for the five years while I'm saving the other varieties I grow.

The Unintended Cross!

This is one of the most common reasons amazing gardeners give for not saving seed: "Well, I just want to know I have good seed." Fair. But they are missing out. First of all, if you're reading this book, you'll have many of the tools you need to keep crosses from happening. Nevertheless, I would also suggest that if you haven't had some unintended crosses in your garden, you haven't done enough seed saving. Like pests and bad weather, it's just part of the terrain.

It is very difficult for beans to cross (see section on Legumes: Peas and Beans). A number of sources suggest a minimal separation of about 12 yards is sufficient to prevent unintended crossing. For a variety of reasons, I typically grow all of my different types of beans in adjacent rows. Effectively no separation. And I never get crosses.

The funny thing about "never"—there is really no such thing. Scientists typically don't even use the word—they'll just say "very, very unlikely." Imagine beans that "never" cross, except maybe one in a million. How many bean plants do you think there might be in a five-acre field? 10-acre? 100-acre? That one in a million doesn't seem so unlikely anymore, especially after many years.

While I don't have five acres of beans, I did have a cross—once. My big pink cranberry beans with red specks, grown right next to small black beans, once yielded a few medium grey beans with

The best example of alternating years in a non-perishable crop is field corn or popcorn. If you have two varieties you wish to grow out for seed, just grow one each year, but enough to last for two years. This has the added advantage of giving you a little more space to save a larger population, as you can grow, say, 200 plants of each of two varieties in alternating years, instead of 100 plants of both every year.

5. **Caging.** Caging is an important technique used by seed savers to isolate several different varieties of the same plant in a relatively confined space while avoiding crossing. The "cage" is a fine mesh screen that excludes pollinators. You do have to let pollinators in,

black specks. Honestly, they were beautiful. Were I a plant breeder, I would have been tempted to try and grow them out as a new variety. As it is, I like the beans I grow. So, I threw them in the chili pot with the other beans and used my seed stock from the prior year (always a good idea to keep a few of those around) and I continue to grow them side by side.

One question I always ask folks about this bean example when I'm speaking is, "What year did that cross occur, and when did it show up?" If I grew black and red beans side by side in 2010, 2011, and 2012, and planted the seed from the previous year and subsequent year, and I noticed the grey speckled beans in 2013, which year did the cross take place?

You got it, 2012. It is tempting to think it occurred in 2013, but it occurred the year prior. This is an important question because, which year's seed do I have to go back to in order to get the pure seed? Yes, the year before the cross, or 2011. This is a good rule of thumb that usually works well, though there are a few plants that, due to some complex genetics, may show a cross in the first year. Corn will apparently do this, though I have never witnessed it myself. The bottom line is that it is always a good idea to save some seed for a few years, especially if you are working with a difficult-to-replace variety.

however, or you won't get seeds. You do this by removing the cages from similar plants on alternate days, or by introducing larval pollinators (that is, maggots) into the cage where they will pollinate exclusively that variety. This is an advanced technique that we will not cover in greater detail here.

Crosses with plants outside your garden. Before we leave the issue of maintaining seed purity, there is one more important issue to address, and it happens to be the one issue about which you have the least control: crossing with plants outside your garden. For many home gardeners, this is typically a neighbor's garden. What to do? While you can and should use some of the techniques discussed above (cross-resistant plants and hand pollination are particularly effective here), one of the best techniques is to knock on your neighbor's door, invite him/her/them over for the frosted beverage of your choice, and talk gardening. At the least, you'll find out what they like to grow and will trade pointers on pests. At best, you might find yourself a seed saving partner. If you both save seed, you could collaborate your efforts. Many plants give you more seed than you'll ever need to use. Maybe you'll grow some, your neighbor will grow others, and you'll join together in an order for the rest. Rural and agriculture communities have worked like this for centuries—and for good reason.

Another source of crossing is wild (or feral) plants (the difference between wild and feral is that the latter are domesticated plants that have found their way into the environment and are propagating themselves year after year). Queen Anne's lace is a common issue here. This is wild carrot. It has white, fibrous, not-so-tasty roots, and will pass that trait along to any carrot seeds you allow it to pollinate. What's more, Queen Anne's lace is pretty ubiquitous, particularly in pastures, roadsides, and median strips. I've gone so far as to pull up every plant of it that I can find for a half a mile in every direction, and still it has found a way into my carrot seed. As we go through each variety, I will be sure to list any potential wild species that can affect the purity of your seed.

PART III

If It's Your First Time

Easy Inbreeding Plants with Perfect Flowers

These are some of the easiest of all vegetables to save seed from. For some of them, there is nothing more to do than pluck the seed and bring it inside until next spring. That said, understanding some of the nuance with these easier garden characters will make some of the plants with more complex personalities a bit easier to understand.

A. Peas and Beans

Peas and beans are probably the easiest seeds to save in your garden, for all of the reasons listed above. In the simplest terms, when you grow dry beans (say, a black or pinto bean), your food crop is just your seed crop. All done! Just plant it out next year!

Peas and Beans

Vegetative or Sexual Propagation?	Sexual
Hybrid or Open-Pollinated?	Several excellent open-pollinated varieties available
Annual or Biennial?	Annual
Location of Male/Female Parts	Perfect flower (both on the same flower)
Inbreeding or Outbreeding?	Inbreeding
How Does Pollen Get to Female Part?	Directly from the male part of the same flower
Are There Factors That Affect Purity?	Very low risk of crossing due to very late-opening flower

The reason peas and beans are so easy is that not only is there a perfect flower that is receptive to its own pollen, but those flower parts become fertile prior to the flower opening itself to pollinators. Sure, after the flower opens up, you will see insects visiting, but it's too late. Pollination has occurred. The pregnancy is already achieved. For this reason, it is possible to save different varieties of peas and beans right next to each other with very, very low chance of crossing. (For a description of what can happen when you do get a cross, see The Unintended Cross! in the previous section.)

A few things to consider here. While the food and seed crop are identical in dry beans and soup peas (that is, the thing you eat is the thing you plant), snap peas and green beans are a little different. You need to let them dry down. I typically don't find this very difficult to do. I pick a row of green beans for food every three days for a few weeks. Typically by then, I forget about them as some other crop is coming in. A couple of weeks later I come back and there are several beans that have "gone by"—too tough and fibrous to eat, but starting to set nice, plump seeds. I pull of most of the row at this point as I need the space to plant a late-sum-

Shortly before beans are fully ripe, we like to cut plants right at the soil level and hang them to dry. This keeps beans from sprouting and rotting on damp soil.

mer crop—maybe some chard. I leave a half a dozen bean plants on the end of the row and forget about them until early September. By then, there will be nice dry pods that I can pick off the plant, hand thresh (see Threshing and Winnowing), and store for next season's planting. Peas are similar, but because I grow them along the garden fence, space is less of an issue. With snap peas, for example, I just grow a food crop and pick as many as I can find all July. When they seem to give up in the late July heat, I let them be for a while. In late August, I go back and look for every pea pod I missed, which at this point have dried down into nice little seed packs. Again, I hand thresh and save for future planting.

The biggest enemy of peas and beans—besides maybe squirrels and chipmunks—are late-summer rains. I discuss strategies for addressing this in the section A Drying House (see page 81). Another way to address this is by growing pole beans. Nice and high up, these beans are typically able to dry out given the improved air circulation, rather than lying on the ground and rotting (or sprouting!) like their bush kin.

B. Lettuce

One year we got a cool, prolonged spring with a nice even amount of rain. We had a fantastic stand of lettuce heads that year. Because we only had a small garden at the time, we were picking a few leaves of the outside of each plant every night, in hopes that we could get our half-dozen or so plants to keep giving us greens into the early summer.

Lettuce

Vegetative or Sexual Propagation?	Sexual
Hybrid or Open-Pollinated?	Typically open-pollinated
Annual or Biennial?	Annual
Location of Male/Female Parts	Perfect flower (both on the same flower)
Inbreeding or Outbreeding?	Inbreeding—flower receptive to its own pollen
How Does Pollen Get to Female Part?	Directly from the male part of the same flower
Are There Factors That Affect Purity?	Very low risk of crossing

In late June, just as it was getting hot, we went hiking in Alaska for two weeks. When we came back, we had lettuce seed ripening in the July sun.

That's pretty much how it works. You can plant different varieties right next to each other. Warmer and drier weather induces lettuces to bolt into stalks about three feet high. Flowers will emerge at the top of the stalk, and will set little bunches of seed attached to bits of fuzz (like a dandelion, though they are better about staying in their packets rather than flying away). When they dry down (or when they are almost dry, if you are about to have a lot of rain), cut the stalk at the base and hang upside down in a safe space to allow to fully dry out. Don't wait for all of the *tillers* (these are smaller stalks coming off of the main seed stalk) to have dry seed on them—by then the seed from your main stalk will have fallen and sprouted. Once the hanging seed stalk has dried, rub the dry seed head between your palms over a bowl. You will get lots of nice seed and a lot of *chaff* (dried up bits of leaves and so on), too. Outside, gently swirl the bowl as you blow over the surface. The chaff will blow away, you'll see some of the seed blow away too, but as long as you aren't blowing like a gale, these are just infertile seeds that are OK to lose. The nice, heavy, fertile seeds will fall to the bottom of the

In short season climates like New England, set out lettuce for seed early in the spring, with plenty of space to grow. The wire fence here will make a nice support when the seed stalks emerge.

bowl. You don't need to keep blowing until it is as clean as commercial seed (the one exception might be if you are planning on planting with a fancy commercial seeder). Just do this until it is clean enough for you, and store for future planting. Even though this is taking up some precious garden space (your food lettuce is there for 40 days, the seed crop will be there much of the summer), you will get tons of seed from each plant—enough to share with friends and family and keep for yourself for several years. So, you don't have to give up that garden space every year. What's more, lettuce is so inbreeding it will do just fine to save seed from just a few plants.

C. Tomatoes

Like peas, beans, and lettuce, tomatoes are well suited for seed saving in the home garden. You can save excellent seed from a small number of plants with different varieties growing right next to each other. In addition to being inbreeding self-pollinators, this is made possible by the fact that the male part of the flower covers the female part so completely that—if and when the

Tying lettuce plants together once they bolt is a great way to keep them from leaning into the soil and spoiling the ripening seed.

Tomatoes

Vegetative or Sexual Propagation?	Sexual
Hybrid or Open-Pollinated?	Lots of both. Be careful to look!
Annual or Biennial?	Annual
Location of Male/Female Parts	Perfect flower (both on the same flower)
Inbreeding or Outbreeding?	Inbreeding—flower receptive to its own pollen
How Does Pollen Get to Female Part?	Directly from the male part of the same flower
Are There Factors That Affect Purity?	Some crossing on potato-leaf varieties

While difficult to see exactly how the male parts are covering the female part on this tomato flower, it is pretty apparent that you can't see the female part of this flower. For contrast, see the picture of a potato flower below. The female part is the small dark object protruding from the center.

flower is visited by a pollinator—all it does is knock the pollen directly from the male part right into the female part of the same flower. It can't even get to the female part. Cool, right? Like nearly everything in nature, however, there always needs to be an exception, and in this case, it is the potato-leaf varieties of tomatoes.

The leaves of most tomato plants look kind of like oak leaves. There are a few, however, like Brandywine and Pruden's Purple, that have more oval-shaped leaves that look very much like the leaves of a potato plant (hence the name). In addition to this unusual shape, these varieties have longer-than-usual female flower parts that stick out above the male parts. These promiscuous varieties are at risk of being pollinated by outsiders and require a little separation from other tomatoes. This is just an issue for that tomato, though, not for the other ones. You could grow a Brandywine next to a Purple Cherokee and a Yellow Pear, and the latter two will not have a problem.

Once you have a ripe tomato (this could be one that is vine ripened, or one picked in that "almost ripe" state and allowed to ripen on the window sill), the next step is to ferment the seed. This is not difficult at all, but it *is* necessary for two reasons. First, you probably have noticed that the seeds in a tomato are surrounded by a little membrane that makes them look like a frog's egg. This must be fermented off so that the seed can be properly stored. Second, the fermentation prevents transmission of a number of tomato diseases, including the much-feared late blight, among others.

To do the fermentation, squeeze some seeds along with some tomato juice into a small jar. For very dry past tomatoes, I sometimes add just a little bit of water. Place the jar, uncovered, in a place out of direct sunlight where it won't be disturbed. I like a north-east facing window. The next step I recommend is telling your spouse, partner, or other housemate what you are up to, because I've lost more than one jar of fermenting seed to the diligent kitchen cleaning of my wife. (How can I complain, really, when she's the one that cleaned up dinner that night!). Speaking of spouses, they are often the ones that will tell you when the fermentation is done—because a green film will appear on the surface of the liquid and it will start to smell a little. This will take 3–5 days. If you leave them in too long, the danger is that they can start to sprout. I've not had this issue leaving them there up to 7 days, but if you have the time and the seeds are done, there's no reason to wait.

To finish the job, take the jar of fermented seed, add a little water, and stir with a fork to make sure the seeds are well separated from the other material (this is often unnecessary if the fermentation is complete). Then pour off most of the water. Most of the seeds will go to the bottom while the fermented solids can be poured off the top. You will pour off a few seeds, too, but like in our lettuce seeds that we blow into the wind, these will generally not be the healthy, viable seeds that you want. Add some more water to the mixture and repeat this 3–4 times until the water runs clear. Then pour off as much water as you can and pour the damp seeds out onto a plate to dry. You'll want to separate them while they are still damp, because once they dry it will be very difficult to do so. I just put them on a dinner plate on top of the fridge,

Peppers

Vegetative or Sexual Propagation?	Sexual
Hybrid or Open-Pollinated?	Check your variety. Many classic sweet peppers are hybrids
Annual or Biennial?	Annual
Location of Male/Female Parts	Perfect flowers
Inbreeding or Outbreeding?	Inbreeding
How Does Pollen Get to Female Part?	Direct transfer, similar to tomato. Some insect pollination
Are There Factors That Affect Purity?	Crosses a little more easily than tomato. Hot gene is dominant. Use caution saving sweets next to hots!

and the next morning they are dry. You can dry them on paper towels or newspaper, too, but I find that they stick to those. Once the seeds are all dry, they are ready for storage!

D. Peppers

Of the "easy" plants, peppers are perhaps the most difficult. While inbreeding plants that are receptive to their own pollen and can be grown in small populations, they cross a little more easily than the others listed here. To that end, a word of caution—the gene that makes hot peppers hot is dominant. This means that while a hot pepper cannot be made sweet by the pollen of a sweet pepper, a sweet pepper *will* be made hot with the pollen of a hot pepper. Taste that first pepper with caution! The one pepper I typically save to seed is cayenne. While I grow most of my food peppers in a hothouse on the north end of our yard, I grow one cayenne pepper on the south side of the house, just about thirty yards away, with lots of good stuff for pollinators in between. I've never had a problem.

While peppers don't have to be fermented like tomatoes, you *do* have to make sure that you are saving seed from a ripe pepper. That means not using the seeds from green peppers (unless you have a particular variety that is truly ripe at the green stage). For most peppers this will be red, orange, yellow, purple, etc.

KEEPING IT SIMPLE

1. All of the vegetables discussed in this section can be grown side by side with other similar vegetables with very little chance of crossing, except some potato-leafed tomatoes and some peppers.
2. Dry beans and soup peas are both the food and the seed crop. Just save a few for planting.
3. Green beans and snap peas just need to "go by" the eating stage, get plump, and then be allowed to dry down to be good for seed.
4. Lettuce for seed should be planted in the spring. It will bolt in the hot weather of mid-summer, and set a seed head. When the seed heads are nearly dry, cut and hang in a safe place until fully dry, then thresh and winnow the chaff to get clean seed.
5. Ferment the seeds of ripe tomatoes by placing them with their pulp in a jar for 3–5 days, then rinse clean and dry.
6. Peppers cross a little easier than tomatoes. The hot gene is dominant. Make sure to use ripe (usually not green) peppers.

PART IV

Plants with Moving Parts

In the last chapter, we discussed most of the "easy" seeds to save. This is where most beginning seed saving instruction stops. This is a mistake. So many of us grow zucchini, squash, and pumpkins, that it would be a shame not to give you the tools to save this seed. And while biennials can be a bit tricky, they are in some cases pretty easy to keep from crossing, as you typically harvest your food crop in the first year when there is no flower. In this section, therefore, let's review some of these "more difficult" plants. Taking issue with that label, however, I've called them plants with moving parts.

A. The Squash Family

The squash family is a large group of plants that includes pumpkins, gourds, zucchini, summer squash, winter squash, spaghetti squash, and butternuts. These names we give speak mostly to appearance and culinary use. Biologically speaking, there are five different kinds of squash, though here we will only cover three, as these constitute the bulk of squash grown for food and decor.

Cucurbita pepo—Perhaps the largest species, this includes zucchini and summer squash like yellow crookneck and patty pan. (The term "summer squash" is really a culinary term for squash we eat in their tender, immature state.) This also includes winter squash like spaghettis, acorns, and delicatas, as well as pumpkins like New England Pie and Howden.

Cucurbita maxima—These are buttercups, kabochas, hubbards, and some pumpkins, like Big Max and Cinderella pumpkin (Rouge Vif d'Etampes).

Cucurbita moschata—This includes butternut squash as well as some less commonly grown squashes such as cheese pumpkin and a tear-drop-shaped variety named "Seminole." These are my personal favorites, not only for their delicately sweet flavor but also because they are resistant to squash vine borers—the demon feared by all squash.

The practical result of this confusing categorization is important: you can grow one *pepo*, one *maxima*, and one *moschata* right next to each other in the garden and there will be no crossing. Grow two *pepos* next to each other, however, and they see each other not as different veggies (or fruits, rather), but as partners in reproduction. Sex partners. We should be reassured, however, by two things: 1) there are some easy techniques to avoid unintended crossings, and 2) this apparent lack of discrimination between two individuals that looks so different on the surface is just the kind of thing the world needs more of these days.

Let's look at three different techniques for growing these seeds out without unintended crossing.

Squash Family

Vegetative or Sexual Propagation?	Sexual
Hybrid or Open-Pollinated?	Several excellent open-pollinated varieties available
Annual or Biennial?	Annual
Location of Male/Female Parts	Male and female parts on different flowers on the same plant
Inbreeding or Outbreeding?	On the fence. Will accept own pollen at times, does much better accepting pollen from another plant. Does well in smaller populations
How Does Pollen Get to Female Part?	Insect pollination
Are There Factors That Affect Purity?	Crossing within but not between three (or five) different species of squash. See description

1. Just let them grow. This technique is useful if you really are only growing one from each variety. It is typically most useful for *Cucurbita moschata*, or butternut squashes. I mean, how many different varieties of butternuts can one family grow? Even if I have a close neighbor who is growing a different strain of butternut than I am, I'm not going to be too fussed if there is some crossing. If you are lucky enough to be isolated from other squash growers by a few hundred yards, and you are only growing one of each species, you can just let the pollinators do their work and you should get good results.

2. Spacing. This is an option if you want to grow a few different varieties of each and you've got some space: 200–300 yards of separation is typically sufficient, but as noted elsewhere, this depends on what else you have growing in that space and just how disastrous (or not) a cross would be.

3. Hand pollination. For most home gardeners in a situation where they can't "Just let them grow," this is usually the best option. Therefore, we will discuss in some detail below.

Hand-pollinating squash

The first step in hand pollination is to be able to tell the male from the female flower. This is pretty straightforward, as the female flower will have a miniature fruit at the base (it will look like a tiny version of the full-size squash), whereas the male flower will not.

Once you have identified the male and female flowers, the next step is to go out in the early evening and see if you can identify those flowers that will open the next morning. They will be green and closed but starting to plump up. You might be able to see a rim of the yellow flower starting to emerge in the cracks that will separate the petals. Once you are comfortable that you can identify the flower the night before it opens, you'll want to put a small paper bag over it and tie this off at the bottom with a piece of garden twine. Why, you ask? Unless you plan to get started before the bees the next morning (don't lie to yourself) this is an important step to make sure they don't get their dirty little parts all over your nice clean flower. Make sure to bag several

male flowers for every female flower (if there aren't enough around, just wait and go out another night). While squash will accept their own pollen to some degree, they are much happier getting pollen from another plant, so be sure to include more than one plant.

The next morning, take the bags off the male flowers. If you have identified them correctly they will have opened. If you removed the petals, what remains in the center will look like...well, it will look like a male part. I will say no more on that, as the next step is to rip the flower off by the base (please apologize to the plant as you do this). If you look closely, it will be full of yellow dust. You then take that over to one of the female flowers you had covered. Gently dab the pollen from the male flower onto the protruding parts of the female flower. Once you are satisfied that you have done a good job spreading the pollen, do the same with another male flower on the same female flower. This ensures good, thorough pollination—remember we're taking all the responsibil-

See how the female flower of these two squashes (pumpkin above, zucchini below) look like minature versions of the grown-up fruit. The pumpkin flower is shown the day prior to opening. This one should be bagged in the evening if we intend to hand pollinate in the morning. See more detailed pictures on squash pollination in the color section.

ity for that as we'll be excluding pollinators! I get good results using three male flowers to each female flower. If you are in a pinch and can just use one, fine. After you are done, there is one more step before you cover the flower back up, and that is to mark it somehow. You won't be hand-pollinating every fruit, so you'll want to know which fruits you've done, so you can use those ones for seed and eat the rest. You can use a red twist tie or a piece of string. My friend Will Bonsall likes to use a safety pin to scratch a shallow X in the side of the small fruit. Once grown, there will be a large X-shaped scar on the side of the fruit, clearly indicating it as part of the seed crop. However you do it, once the fruit is marked, carefully replace the bag over the female flower so that it is not visited by any pollinators later that day. By the next day, you can remove the bag. She is either pregnant or not, and nothing any pollinator will do that day will change the matter. If the fruit aborts, don't worry. That happens. Just try again with another set of flowers.

Once you feel comfortable that you are avoiding unintended crossing, the only issue is to make sure that you are saving the seed from mature fruit. This is primarily an issue for summer squash, which as noted before is simply squash that is eaten in an immature state. You need to let the summer squash grow out until they look like winter squash before you harvest the seed. This can be pretty fun. Have you ever gone out of town in the late summer only to find monster zucchinis waiting for you when you return? Those are the ones you leave on the plant for seed. The only problem is that once the plant perceives that it has produced a good seed crop, its production of new zucchinis may slow down or stop. For most of us, however, there comes a time point in late summer where, honestly, this is a welcome phenomenon.

I recall once bringing in two huge zucchinis from the garden to use for seed. I left them in our downstairs window to cure (squash seeds need to after-ripen a bit to be at their best). An hour later they were gone. "What did you do with my zucchinis?" I asked my wife. She responded with one raised eyebrow, as if to say, "You think I have nothing better to do than go hiding your zucchinis on you?" "Right," I replied. Just then, my two girls called out from upstairs. "Daddy, come look."

There, in their bedroom, tucked gently into bed next to their baby dolls, were two huge zucchini babies, swaddled gently in the girls' own baby blankets. This was a fine activity while they cured. A month later, the seed was put out to dry and the flesh fed to the chickens. My girls are much older now, but please don't tell them the fate of their poor zucchini "baby dolls." They've never asked, and I'm afraid they'd be upset.

One last thing we should discuss is what to do with the seed. This is not complicated. Like other seed, you just need to make sure it is dry before you put it away; see the sidebar on Curing Seed, Seed Storage, and Longevity. Simply remove it from the seed cavity, set it out on a plate in an airy place, and let it dry for a week or two. Make sure it is in a single layer, or else it can be prone to mold. If you have a lot of seed, like for a pumpkin, spread it out on cookie trays. This is also how we dry pepitas—naked (hull-less) pumpkin seeds to put on salads—the best-kept secret of the pumpkin world.

B. Spinach

I first started growing spinach to seed because I wanted to see the difference between the male and female plants. I mean, how cool that a plant can be "male or female," something that we are tempted to think of as a purely animal trait. (That said, there are other male or female plants; asparagus and holly are two.) While spinach does alright genetically speaking with a smallish population (say 25 plants), because it is

Spinach

Vegetative or Sexual Propagation?	Sexual
Hybrid or Open-Pollinated?	Most of the newer varieties are hybrid, be sure to check
Annual or Biennial?	Annual
Location of Male/Female Parts	Each plant has all male or all female parts
Inbreeding or Outbreeding?	Outbreeding
How Does Pollen Get to Female Part?	Wind pollination
Are There Factors That Affect Purity?	Different varieties cross

wind-pollinated, you can get pretty poor pollination if you don't use at least two dozen or so plants. Fortunately, spinach plants are relatively small, so it is a lot easier to save 25 spinaches to seed than, say, 200 corn plants. The other advantage of spinach is that you can eat a few of the leaves when the plant is young without significantly affecting the seed crop.

Cultivation is very similar to lettuce. Plant in the early spring. Or, better yet, plant in the early fall. It will often overwinter and grow early in the spring (we're treating it a bit like a biennial in doing this, though it is not). Plants will start to bolt as the days get hotter, longer, and drier. Stake them if they get over-large. You can tell the female plants as the flowers grow close to the stalk. As they dry down, cut them at the base, hang them to dry (just the female plants), and thresh and winnow as you would lettuce.

C. Easy(er) Biennials

Biennials are plants that bear seed in their second year. They typically spend their first summer lazily growing large fat tap roots, storing energy to shoot up a seed stalk early in their second year. This is why we don't see seeds for many of our garden vegetables. Quite simply, they never reach sexual maturity, because we eat them in their juvenile state.

Besides the challenge of getting them through a winter alive, biennials also tend to be outbreeders that only do well with a larger population. That said, one nice thing about biennials is that it is much easier to control potential crosses from other plants in your garden (or for that matter, your neighbor's garden!). While growing five different types of peppers in a cluster may be tempting fate in terms of an undesired cross, you can grow dozens of different onions (for food) right together, as long as you're only planting one of them for seed in its second year. (It's unlikely that your neighbor will have any onions in their second year, and if they do, you should definitely have a conversation about how you can collaborate!) For the seed-bearing onion in its second year, all of its pre-adolescent neighbors will be nary a threat to the desired genetic outcome of its offspring!

Given this, there are a few easier biennials that are worth a try, even if you don't have much space to allot to them. I present three here (four including leeks) that I've found to do well with a smaller population, despite being true outbreeders. While we should not be intimidated by these plants in our home gardens, we do have to keep in mind that we are asking them to be something (inbreeders) that they are not. While I've found these plants to do fine, population size is not only important in the first year (in fact, for one year you can often get away with it), but can become a threat in each successive generation thereafter (see the human example in How Deep is Your Gene Pool? in Part II).

How you handle this depends on your purpose in saving seed. If you're saving seed of a common variety for your own use, just go for it. If after a few generations you notice some *inbreeding depression* (less hardy and vigorous plants due to too small a gene pool), chuck the seed and buy new. (Keep in mind some seeds can be saved for over five years—even more in the freezer—so three generations could last you fifteen years or more.) If, on the other hand, you are saving an unreplaceable variety (perhaps a true heirloom you got from family or friends), try and grow as many as you can. If you can spare the room,

Onions and Leeks

Vegetative or Sexual Propagation?	Sexual
Hybrid or Open-Pollinated?	There are a lot of hybrids, so make sure you are working with an open-pollinated variety
Annual or Biennial?	Biennial
Location of Male/Female Parts	Perfect flower (both on the same flower)
Inbreeding or Outbreeding?	Outbreeding (can do well with smaller populations)
How Does Pollen Get to Female Part?	Insect pollination
Are There Factors That Affect Purity?	Onions will cross with other varieties of onions and leeks with leeks. Onions do not cross-pollinate with leeks. Garden leeks do *not* cross with wild leeks (ramps), which are not true leeks.

better to grow fifty plants every third year than five plants every year (from a seed perspective, not for food). That said, better to grow five plants than none at all and let the variety die out.

As you gear up to try these, be sure to read the section on Biennials and Winter Storage (see page 70) for help in getting these plants through the winter.

Onions and Leeks

Onions do so well in a smaller population that I've actually seen them listed in some places as inbreeders. While they cross with each other, as with other biennials, as long as you are only saving one variety for seed per year, this is not a significant concern. (Note: If you want to save multiple onions or other outbreeders for seed, follow instructions in Part III: that is, by significant separation—a few hundred yards or more—or by caging.)

In the first year, grow onions just like you would for food. For northern areas, this means an early start inside, setting them out in late April or early May and keeping them well fed with compost, well weeded, and well watered, especially while forming bulbs. Once the tops fall over in the late summer or early fall, it's time to cure them. Because you'll have to

Sometimes harder-to-store biennials can be "tricked" into going to seed the first year. This swiss chard was started indoors very early, and then set into the garden early in a cold, wet spring. By the time summer arrived, it clearly felt that it had just lived through a winter (albeit a rather mild winter for Vermont) and felt the need to bolt to seed. This was intended as a food crop, and in that sense, is a "failure." A clear win, though, in my efforts to save chard seed!

get your onions through the long winter before setting them out in the second year, make sure you cure them well—just like you will for the storage onions that you will eat. To do so, place the harvested onions on a screen in the sun until the tops are dried down and the skin is dry and tight. Then turn them over. This is best done over a couple weeks, which is why it works best in the greenhouse (no rain or dew), but can be done right out in the garden if needed.

Once dried, onions like to be kept in a cool, dry place: 50 degrees and 50% humidity. In this case, an insulated but unheated basement with a poured concrete foundation works well (again, see the section on Biennials and Winter Storage). Storage onions are pretty easy to get through to spring. Most sweet onions don't keep as well, but sometimes if you put them in your refrigerator crisper you can get them to last.

I am somewhat notorious for giving my poor flowering leeks the most forgotten corner of the garden. The weeds grow, but happily the leeks grow faster and have never disappointed me. This is a relatively small planting of only four plants. We typically do closer to a dozen.

Your biggest job over the winter (and this is where it hurts) is to take your dozen (or ideally more) biggest, most magnificent-looking bulbs, and *not* eat them. These will be the bulbs you set out in the spring. This can be done pretty early on, as soon as the ground can be worked. Remember, in milder climates these would be sitting out through the winter, so a hard frost is typically not an issue here. In Vermont, this is typically in the last week of April. Set them out about eight inches apart, and mulch with some leaves or other material to suppress weeds (this will also provide added low-temperature protection for early spring).

Greens will emerge (if they haven't already started to emerge in storage) and eventually a seed stalk. A round seed head will emerge at the top of the stalk. My mother-in-law often observes that a cluster of a dozen onions or leeks at this stage look very much like a group of people (with the flowers as their heads) trying to peak over the garden fence at something quite interesting. At this point, it is often helpful to stake the stalks, as they will often bend to the ground in heavy rain and wind. Late in the summer, you will notice that if you crush some of the seed clusters, they are full of juicy black seeds. Leave these to dry in place if you can, or—once they seem full but not yet dry—cut and hang the stalks as described in the section A Drying House. You can take a dozen or so stalks and hang them in a single cluster upside down until they are nice and dry. You can thresh and winnow them at this point or, better yet, put them in vase as part of a winter dry flower arrangement until you need them in the spring.

Leeks are done in very much the same way, except that instead of drying and saving a bulb to replant the next year, you need to pull of the whole plant—leaves, roots, and all—and repot to be kept in the root cellar. Your availability of a root cellar-like place to keep your leeks will determine how doable this is for you. If you live in a milder area, leeks, like many other biennials, will overwinter right in the garden, as they are rather cold hardy. That said, they are not quite hardy enough for a true northern winter. To overwinter them inside, use a large plastic pot that a shrub or tree came in from the nursery, or a five-gallon bucket (make sure there are some holes to drain water). Put three inches garden soil or compost in the bottom (some people say sand but I find it too drying). Place about 6–8 leeks in each pot—or as many as will fit—and fill soil in around the plants. The soil should stay moist but not wet. Depending on conditions in the root cellar, you might need to water occasionally a few times during the winter so the leeks do not dry out. Plant them out again in the early spring (they are hardier than onions). Try to do this during a stretch of cloudy or even rainy weather because leeks—unlike onion bulbs—have all of their foliage out there but the roots will not be set right away, a recipe for drying out. All that leaf surface area is a great place to lose moisture. Leeks are surprisingly hardy, so I've seen many of them make it when I've been less gentle with timing than they deserve. That said, it is easier on both you and your leeks to set them out in cooler, cloudy weather. Once they get going and set a seed stalk, treat them just like onions for a seed crop.

Parsley

Parsley is one of the easiest biennials to grow, for a few reasons. First, while technically an outbreeder, it tolerates a small population just fine. I don't think I've ever grown more than 24 parsley plants at once. Second, it is very easy to get through the winter by one of two ways. It can winter right in the ground here in Vermont, especially if there is some snow cover. Better yet, grow it in a pot and bring it inside. You can pick a few leaves to put in your soup all winter long. Sometime in late March you'll notice it start to bolt. Stop picking the leaves, and as soon as it's warm enough for the grass to green up a bit, go ahead and put it in the ground. I grow 3–4 plants in one large pot, and don't separate them when planting them out in the second year. You may have to stake them (or better yet, tie them together). Harvest when seeds are dry, then hand thresh (see section on Threshing and Winnowing). Kept in a cool, dry place, they will continue to germinate for five years or more, and a single year's seed crop will grow more than you can possibly use.

Parsley

Vegetative or Sexual Propagation?	Sexual
Hybrid or Open-Pollinated?	Typically open-pollinated
Annual or Biennial?	Biennial
Location of Male/Female Parts	Perfect flower (both on the same flower)
Inbreeding or Outbreeding?	Outbreeding (tolerates modest inbreeding)
How Does Pollen Get to Female Part?	Insect pollinated
Are There Factors That Affect Purity?	Different varieties will cross

Kale

Kale is part of the cabbage family, which is a bit complex (really, don't we all come from complex families in one way or another?). As long as you are saving just one kale and no cabbage, rutabaga, broccoli, etc., then you are pretty safe from a crossing perspective. If you are growing more than that—or are not sure—see the section on the cabbage family, below. Also, some kales (red kale, for example) aren't true kales. Again, see the section on the cabbage family

As noted in Part I, the first time I saved kale seed it was a total accident. The hardest thing about growing kale for seed in cold climates is getting it through the winter. Unlike parsley, it's not quite as amenable to being brought into the house in a pot, so this generally means overwintering in the garden. Fortunately, kale is one of the most winter-hardy plants we grow in the garden. The main key to this (besides snow cover) is timing. Large plants that have been growing since spring will be nice and hardened off, but they'll be too big to hang out under the snow near the ground, where they are safest from the cold. On the other hand, newish plants started in the fall will be too tender to handle the winter and too small to produce good seed come spring (unless you live in a climate with a mild winter, where this might be just the thing). For most kales here in Vermont, I find an early July start to work quite well.

As with parsley, kale is an outbreeding plant that is supposed to like a breeding population of several dozen to do well. Also like parsley, I find kale does fine with a smaller population. And you can eat some of the lower leaves and still get an excellent seed crop. See more below on Space-Saving Strategies.

Kale

Vegetative or Sexual Propagation?	Sexual
Hybrid or Open-Pollinated?	Some of the most common crinkle-leafed kales are hybrids, though several excellent open-pollinated varieties exist
Annual or Biennial?	Biennial
Location of Male/Female Parts	Perfect flower (both on the same flower)
Inbreeding or Outbreeding?	Outbreeding (tolerates some inbreeding)
How Does Pollen Get to Female Part?	Insect pollination
Are There Factors That Affect Purity?	Different varieties will cross.

KEEPING IT SIMPLE

1. The squash family is divided into various species that will not cross with each other but will cross within that species.
2. The easiest way to grow squash is limiting to one type from each species. This is easiest for moschata. Otherwise, hand pollinate.
3. Summer squash need to mature to their "winter squash" equivalents in order to save seed.
4. Spinach has male and female plants. It does OK in smaller populations but try and use at least 25 plants or so, as it is wind-pollinated.
5. Onions, parsley, and kale are relatively easy biennials to try.
   a. After curing onions in the sun, keep them in a warmish dry basement.
   b. Leeks should be replanted in a bucket, kept in a cold basement, and watered occasionally so they don't dry out.
   c. Kale can often overwinter right in the garden.
   d. Parsley overwinters beautifully on a window sill, and tolerates the harvest of greens for most of the winter.

As the snow melts in the spring at the beginning of the kale's second year in the garden, you will probably notice some leaves that have died back, but you should also notice some nice, young green ones starting to emerge at the top of the plant. If you have no interest in seed saving at this point, this makes a lovely succulent early-spring vegetable. If you only had one or two plants make it through a difficult winter, this is too small a population for a good seed crop, so just go ahead and eat them. Assuming you have at least four or five (again, ideally more) that survived the long winter, however, don't touch that new growth! Like with onions, you will eventually notice that the plant will start to send up a seed stalk that will flower and, eventually, set seed. At this point, what we've said about lettuce applies well. You will likely need to stake these seed stalks, as they can be huge (remember the parable about the mustard seed—mustard is a cousin of kale). Better than staking is to tie three together like a tripod. Again, like with lettuce, a strong rain for several days in a row on drying seed will ruin the crop. So, as the stalk begins to dry down, go ahead and cut it off at the base and hang it upside down in your drying space. Don't wait for all of the tillers to be dry—it will be too late at that point for the center stalk. Thresh and winnow as discussed for lettuce.

Not as Hard as They Look

Biennials and Obligate Outbreeders

A. Corn

Whether or not you can save corn for seed will have a lot to do with where you live and what goes on around you. If you are surrounded by farmers growing fields and fields of corn, good luck. The pollen from their fields will be difficult to keep off of your corn. Not impossible, but your challenges will be significant. If you don't have this problem, saving corn for seed is not quite as intimidating as you have been led to believe.

We are fortunate in our location—while Vermont has many dairy farms that grow corn, none are within a mile or so. As an extra buffer, we are surrounded by a fair amount of forest that provides some additional shelter. Knock on wood, I've never had a problem.

The biggest challenge of saving corn besides wind contamination is population size. As noted above, inbreed depression can be seen in the very first year. Many sources say to save seed produced by a stand of no less than 100–200 plants, though a population as low as 50 can be successful. Five rows of 16 plants (15 x 12 feet) has a respectable population of 80 plants. To maximize genetic diversity of your population, try the following:

1. **Take your seed from the whole crop.** Remember how, when saving squash, we designated which specific fruits we would use for seed? Don't do that with your corn crop. If you set aside an ear or two of

corn to save for seed, that is a tremendous genetic bottleneck. Instead, husk all the corn, remove it from the cob, and collect it in one large container. Mix well. Then take some out for your seed crop. The rest is your food crop.

2. **If space is an issue, grow a larger crop every other year.** We discussed this in Part II when discussing isolation. Not only does this allow you to grow two varieties without crossing, it also allows you a larger population of plants, as you only need room for one variety.

3. **Mix seeds year over year when you plant.** This is something I do that, to be fair, I only have a theoretical basis for doing. When planting a corn crop in year 4, I mix the seed I grew in years 1, 2, and 3. To some degree, this is just a different type of inbreeding (we're mixing parents in with offspring here). However, I believe it does two things. First, if there were individuals that are not represented from the prior year (just because I didn't pick out that seed from that plant) it allows them another chance to be included in the next year's planting. Second, it can avoid genetic bottlenecks. Suppose these are some genes that, for whatever reason, didn't get passed from year 2 to year 3. By including some of the seed crop from

Corn

Vegetative or Sexual Propagation?	Sexual
Hybrid or Open-Pollinated?	Most modern sweet corns are hybrids. There are several excellent open-pollinated popcorns and field corns
Annual or Biennial?	Annual
Location of Male/Female Parts	Male part at tip of stalk. Silks are female part that lead to each kernel
Inbreeding or Outbreeding?	An aggressive outbreeder, needs as big a population as you can give it. Inbreeding depression can be seen in the first generation
How Does Pollen Get to Female Part?	Wind pollination
Are There Factors That Affect Purity?	Tiny pollen grains travel for miles by wind

year 1, I give those genes a chance of representation. Again, this is an experiment. I have had good results, whether due to this practice or in spite of it.

4. **Grow and share corn with a friend.** You can do this in two ways. First, as with growing a crop every other year, you and a friend can each have room for a larger crop, and then share the results with each other. You can grow the field corn and they the popcorn, and split the crops 50/50. If you both grow the same variety of corn, trade a packet of seed with each other and plant of mix of your own and their seed crop. You'll have twice as much genetic diversity that way.

Another challenge of saving corn seed is that, like us, it is very likely that you will want to grow more than one variety. Planting every other year will help, but we grow sweet corn (yes, a hybrid variety) for a food crop every year. Planting every other year won't help us with that. This is a circumstance where separating by time can be very advantageous. For field corn (for corn meal) we grow Painted Mountain—a fantastic, early maturing variety that can be planted in early May in cool soil. Its pollen is released very early, sometimes by early July. We then plant a food crop of sweet corn and a very long-season popcorn, both of which go into the ground in late May or early June. By the time the sweet corn is sending out its pollen, the field corn is already set. Likewise, the popcorn is so late, by the time its silks are looking for pollen, the sweet corn is done. If it looks close (like there is still an active stalk or two of sweet corn lingering and sending out pollen), I simply cut the top off of the sweet corn plant (the ear will continue to ripen). Suffice it to say, this is a bit easier to pull off in a region with a longer growing season. Even in our northern climate, however, if you choose the right varieties, you can work the timing to your advantage.

Finally, like we've said with our other seed varieties, they have to be dry for storage. You can pick the ears before they are fully dry if you must. We often do this for our popcorn—sometimes due to an early hard freeze (a light frost is a non-issue for viable seed that is just drying down), and sometimes due to hungry squirrels. In this case, I recommend husking the cobs and setting them out on racks to dry (inaccessible to squirrels). If you don't husk them and they are not quite dry, they can mold. Once the cobs are dry, remove the kernels from the cob by twisting them in your hand. I recommend a pair of leather work gloves—after a few dozen ears they will save the skin on your hands. If the kernels are reluctant to release, let them dry another week or two. Kept cool and dry, open-pollinated corn seed stores for a very long time.

B. Carrots and Parsnip

Carrots would decidedly be in the "easier biennial" section if it weren't for one thing—Queen Anne's lace. This is discussed in detail in the section Crosses with Plants Outside Your Garden. In brief, this is a wild version of carrot that will cross readily with your carrots. The result is that the offspring will be tiny and tough. (Not that there is anything wrong with being tiny and tough, as we are decidedly a family of cross-country runners and not linebackers, but it's not really what we want out of our carrots.)

If you don't have Queen Anne's lace in your area (if you aren't sure, ask around—people will know, and it's not hard to spot) you should

Carrots and Parsnips

Vegetative or Sexual Propagation?	Sexual
Hybrid or Open-Pollinated?	Several excellent open-pollinated varieties available
Annual or Biennial?	Biennial
Location of Male/Female Parts	Perfect flower (both on the same flower)
Inbreeding or Outbreeding?	Outbreeding
How Does Pollen Get to Female Part?	Insect pollination
Are There Factors That Affect Purity?	Queen Anne's lace (wild carrot) and wild (or rather, feral) parsnip are crossing challenges

This motley crew is doing a great job with the fall carrot harvest. If you are going to save some for seed and your winter is mild enough to overwinter in the garden (doable for us in Vermont for parsnips consistently, but for carrots only in a heavy snow year), make sure to keep a foot or so of spacing between each root that you leave—they are much bigger the second year. This goes double for parsnip.

definitely try carrots. Plant them as you would for food in the first year. Keep them in the root cellar for the winter (see the section Biennials and Winter Storage on page 70). When digging them out at the end of the first year, be sure not to damage the crown, or where the root and the greens meet. You can (and should) cut off most of the greens— these will just rot anyway.

Early in spring the second year (you really can't do this too early), plant the carrots out with a little more space. They like a foot or more, but if space is an issue, it's OK to give them a little less. At a six-inch spacing, they will feel a little crowded, and will probably produce less seed per plant, but this is still to your advantage if it means that you can put out more plants. The plants will bolt, flower, and go to seed as described in the section on Lettuce, though to be honest, it is easier to dry down carrot than lettuce seed. Dry and thresh as described.

Parsnip is very similar to carrot, with only a few differences that actually make it a bit easier. While there is wild (or rather, feral) parsnip, this is not as much of a nuisance to seed savers as is Queen Anne's lace (QAL). First of all, it is less widespread. Second, unlike a carrot crossing with QAL (which is a disaster for the food potential of the offspring), a cross with garden and feral parsnip may not be so bad, as the feral parsnip has typically retained many of its eating qualities. It might not look like that if you pull one up from the ground, but remember, it's not exactly growing in garden conditions. In fact, we have some that look pretty good down on our road that are basically growing out of gravel.

The other nice thing about growing parsnip is that it is supremely winter-hardy. You don't really need to dig it up and put it in the root cellar. In fact, I don't recommend it, as the roots are so long and difficult to remove from the ground in full.

One challenge with parsnip is that some folks are sensitive to the foliage. The plant that we know in New England as "poison parsnip" is really just parsnip. Once on the skin, the oil from the leaf undergoes a reaction with the sun that causes a blistering rash that can be painful. If you have this sensitivity, wear gloves, don't touch your face with them, and wash your hands, gloves, and clothes to remove the oil after you've been handling them.

Otherwise, culture like carrots, except the seeds are more prone to blowing away if you aren't on top of when they are getting ripe!

C. The Cabbage Family

Like the squash family, the cabbage family includes a number of different species that don't cross with each other. That said, the genetics of the cabbage family are even more complex and subtle. I will provide enough information here for those who would like to give saving brassica a try.

Brassica oleracea—True cabbage, collards, kale, kohlrabi, Brussels
 sprouts, broccoli, cauliflower

Brassica napus—Siberian kale, rapeseed, and canola

Brassica rapa—Turnip, Chinese cabbage, broccoli raab (aka rapini)

Brassica napobrassica—Sometimes listed as a subspecies of *napus*; rutabaga (careful, some of the tastiest rutabagas—including Gilfeather—are often called turnips)

Brassica juncea—Mustard

Other: Many Asian greens are subspecies of either *rapa* or *oleracea*. If you are saving more than one, be sure to check the species.

OK, at this late stage in the book, I have to come out and admit something a bit uncomfortable. It's not easy, but here goes. I lied. Back in the very beginning of the book, I told you that once I had a dozen or so kale plants live through the winter. This is a complete falsehood, as it was Siberian kale. "What?" you ask. "I see no material falsehood." For those of us who are growing these vegetables simply for food, it is true there is no practical distinction (though I once read an account where someone said that they could, in fact, *taste* the *napus* in Siberian kale, which I found astonishing). For those of us growing these out for seed, however, it makes all of the difference in the world! In fact, they are two different species of plant—one being *B. oleracea* (true kale) and the other being *B. napus* (Siberian kale). To that end, I could grow one Siberian kale and one true kale for seed in the same year, and have no fear of crossing, but *not* one true kale and a kohlrabi or a cabbage.

Cabbage Family

Vegetative or Sexual Propagation?	Sexual
Hybrid or Open-Pollinated?	Both open-pollinated and hybrid varieties available
Annual or Biennial?	Biennial (some are annuals)
Location of Male/Female Parts	Perfect flower (both on the same flower)
Inbreeding or Outbreeding?	Outbreeding
How Does Pollen Get to Female Part?	Insect pollination
Are There Factors That Affect Purity?	Crossing within different species, but not between them (see description below). Brassica weeds—mostly mustards

Besides keeping the species straight (which will tell you who crosses with whom), the most complicated thing is, again, getting these plants (those that are biennial, anyway) through the winter. Again, in milder climates this is easy, as most of these are very winter-hardy and will make it through a mild winter. Some—particularly the kales and Siberian kale—can make it through a severe winter with adequate snow cover (I've tried mulching with dry leaves, but it doesn't work as well as snow). The root crops are easiest to bring inside. Pull turnips and rutabagas in the late fall, trim away the leaves (taking care not to harm the crown), keep them in the cellar as with carrots (see the section on Biennials and Winter Storage), and plant out again in the early spring. They will need a bit more space in that second year, as the seed stalks can get really big. Brassica crops are generally outbreeders, though I've seen some literature noting that *napus* can tend to inbreeding (which I have to say was borne out in my Siberian kale example). While two-foot spacing for each plant in the second year may be ideal, if space is limited, I'd err on the side of including more plants (to have a bigger population), even if the plants will be a bit cramped.

Cabbage can be a bit tricky to overwinter, but it is also amazingly hardy. The key there is that you will be OK when planting it back out if the roots are moist and green (which is why it seems to work best when replanted inside pots, like leeks, though unlike leeks you can't fit a dozen into one bucket). The leaves around the head of the cabbage may rot, but the heart inside may still be green and ready to grow. Even when the heart of the cabbage appears to have rotted, I've had tillers shoot out from the side, like a phoenix bursting from its ashes. Cabbage's will to live is

KEEPING IT SIMPLE

1. Corn likes a big population and crosses easily with other nearby varieties. However, there are a number of techniques that make this one worth a try.
2. Carrots are easy biennials except that they cross with Queen Anne's lace. They need to be brought inside in the harshest climates and replanted in the next year.
3. Parsnips are similar to carrots, except they can winter pretty well right in place, even in a harsh climate.
4. The cabbage family is a large and diverse group with crossing within but not between species, similar to squash.

truly inspiring in this way. While you can set it out quite early as it is very cold hardy, remember that, coming out, some of these emerging tender parts may not be quite as cold hardy as they were when you first put the thing into the cellar in the fall. They will also be blanched (that is, quite pale, almost white), so they may not appreciate a lot of direct sunlight at first. Cool, damp, cloudy weather is a cabbage's friend in these conditions, at least for the first week or so. Turnips and rutabagas, with those big fat roots, are much less of a concern in this regard. As long as the crown is healthy, they have stored plenty in that big fat root to push out new leaves and new feeder roots.

As with kale (described above) a seed stalk will emerge, flower, and then set seed. It will then begin to dry down and can be threshed and winnowed by hand relatively easily.

Some other things to consider with brassicas:

1. Broccoli is typically classified as a biennial, but practically speaking is an annual. Remember, you are harvesting the florets as food. Tell me with a straight face you've never had some go to flower.

2. There are a number of weeds that are brassicas. Most of these are in the mustard species (*B. juncea*) so will not be an issue for crossing when growing *oleracea* or other species.

3. You will get a *lot* of seed. To that end, consider sprouting some over the winter. I had a rosemary plant die just this past year (I left it out in the frost—just too much to do). It was so sad to see its empty pot, still filled with soil, sitting in its usual spot in the window. So, I decided the use the space by planing Siberian kale seed nice and thick and growing microgreens. Often this can feel like a waste of seed, but when you get as much as you do with the brassicas, it's a great option.

I sound like a broken record here, but this all sounds very complicated. It really isn't. Just give it a try. After the kale (assuming it overwinters in your garden), turnips and rutabagas are probably the simplest to grow (as they are easiest to overwinter).

PART VI

What Have We Missed?

In order to start beginning seed savers with the easiest seeds to save first, I have organized this book by difficulty level (which is admittedly subjective) rather than by botanical classification. As such, there are a few plants that I have not yet included that you may want to know how to save. Now that you know the fundamentals, however, we will cover many of these here in relatively short order.

A. Cucumbers

What veggie says summer more than fresh cucumbers? The biggest issue is that, similar to zucchini, cucumbers are eaten as immature fruits. You have to keep them until they are fully mature to get good seed.

Cucumbers

Vegetative or Sexual Propagation?	Sexual
Hybrid or Open-Pollinated?	Lots of open-pollinated varieties available
Annual or Biennial?	Annual
Location of Male/Female Parts	Male and female part on separate flowers.
Inbreeding or Outbreeding?	Inbreeding—tolerates small population well
How Does Pollen Get to Female Part?	Insect pollination
Are There Factors That Affect Purity?	Will cross-pollinate

Then the seeds and pulp should be scooped out and fermented like tomato seeds, only it's a bit bigger of an operation because the seeds are bigger!

B. Melons

Muskmelons are more closely related to the cucumber (both are the *Cucumis* genus) than the watermelon (genus *Citrullus*). However, unlike cucumber, both muskmelons and watermelons are eaten in their mature state, which is good for the home gardener as you don't have to sacrifice your food crop to save the seed. Nor is fermentation typically done, as it is with cucumber. Varieties of muskmelon will cross-pollinate with other muskmelons, and watermelons with watermelons, so your primary challenge for seed saving will be seeing what your neighbors are growing for a few hundred yards around.

Melons

Vegetative or Sexual Propagation?	Sexual
Hybrid or Open-Pollinated?	Lots of open-pollinated and hybrid varieties available. Check your source for which you have!
Annual or Biennial?	Annual
Location of Male/Female Parts	Male and female parts on separate flowers
Inbreeding or Outbreeding?	Will tolerate a smaller population
How Does Pollen Get to Female Part?	Insect pollination
Are There Factors That Affect Purity?	Muskmelons will not cross-pollinate with watermelons

C. Sunflowers

The biggest barrier to saving sunflower seeds are the squirrels and birds who eat the seeds. Take a piece of light cloth (a piece of old white T-shirt will do) and tie around the pollinated flower head with a piece of string. Because critters are more on the ball than I am, I tend to do

Sunflowers

Vegetative or Sexual Propagation?	Sexual
Hybrid or Open-Pollinated?	Lots of open-pollinated varieties available
Annual or Biennial?	Annual
Location of Male/Female Parts	Male and female parts on same flower
Inbreeding or Outbreeding?	Outbreeding, but tolerates smaller population well
How Does Pollen Get to Female Part?	Insect pollination
Are There Factors That Affect Purity?	Will cross-pollinate

this very early, like before the center of the flower is fully pollinated, because by then I'm probably already losing seed on the edge.

Sunflowers will cross easily with any other sunflower for 400 yards or more, but unless you have a really unique sunflower you are growing, just save them, grow them out, and see what comes.

PART VII

Strategies for Success

A. Curing Seed, Seed Storage, and Longevity

Curing is a fancy way of saying drying down your seed. You cannot put your seeds away until they are dry. Otherwise, they will lose vigor (at best) or mold (at worst). We could find data from the seed saving literature that says seeds should be 12–13% moisture, or whatever, but what does that mean to us home gardeners? There are two easy ways to tell if your seed is ready for storage. The first is that if you are hanging a seed stalk to dry (see A Drying House) and it is dry enough to thresh (see Threshing and Winnowing), then it's pretty likely that it is dry enough to store. Insufficiently dried stems and leaves won't thresh, nor will the seed pods break open during threshing. If all that happens appropriately, your seed is ready to store.

Another way to tell is what I call the ping test. This is useful mostly for larger seed—peas, beans, corn, squash, and the like. Take a metal mixing bowel from your kitchen. Drop the seed inside so it hits the edge. If there is a ping, the seed can be stored. If there is a dull plunk, dry it down some more. I should disclose here that I am a little over the top when it comes to drying my seed—once it passes the ping test, I put it on a high shelf for another week or two until I am sure, then I put it away. One thing you should *not* do is put your seed in a food dehydrator or something similar. While they need to be dry, they are still

We store our seed in a dark closet in an unheated "guestroom."

alive! Don't desiccate your beautiful babies! It turns out the inside of a home in fall with the wood stove on (or central heat, for that matter) is a wonderful place to let your seeds dry on a dinner plate on a high shelf (away from dogs and children). They will wait there patiently for you to put them away.

The keys to good storage are dry seeds in dark, cool, dry conditions. We keep our seeds in paper packets in a large box in the closet in a guest room that goes (somewhat) unheated. It's probably 55–60 degrees in there most of the winter. Of course, this is not perfect, as it is warmer there in the summer, but seed has stored pretty well for us there. Basements are typically too damp. Avoid attics that have extremes in temperatures and humidity. Some of our larger seed stock (beans and such) are stored in mason jars in that same closet. I always have some concern about leaving my seeds in sealed jars—while dormant, they do breathe, believe it or not, just very, very slowly. I haven't had any problems, so I'm probably making too much of things here.

How long you can store seed depends not only on the conditions, but on the type of seed you are saving. Some seeds (onion, leek, and parsnip, for example), last only a year, maybe two. Most other seeds last somewhere in the 3–5-year range. Some, notably grains and particularly corn, can last almost indefinitely if properly stored. Use this information not just for the seed you save, but for the seed you buy. For many things, you won't use a whole packet of seed in the first year. Kept cool and dry, you can use it for a few years. One caveat: F1 hybrids don't last as long. All the more reason to grow open-pollinated and save your own seed!

Make sure to label seeds with the name of the variety and the year grown.

If you have older seed and you aren't sure if it is good, do a germination test. Fold ten or so seeds into a paper towel or newspaper, and keep it consistently moist. Keep it at the right temperature for germinating that seed (60 degrees for onion and cabbage family, 80 degrees for peppers, and 70 degrees for everything else is a good rule of thumb, I find). Check every few days, and after a week or so you'll have a good sense of how viable your seed is. Keep in mind, you need to use at least ten seeds, because viability is not an all-or-nothing thing. It starts dropping off slowly, then rapidly, so using one or two won't give you a good answer.

One technique can be used to greatly prolong your seeds' longevity, and that is freezing. A few important points here: drying is an absolute must, as ice crystals in incompletely dried seed will ruin it. Similarly, seed that is not exquisitely well sealed will dry out in a freezer. The seals must be tight. Finally, retrieving your seed will threaten the longevity of your stock, as opening the container to remove seed will introduce moisture in the form of condensation. To address this, use small plastic bags to store several year-sized amounts of seed in a larger container.

B. Biennials and Winter Storage

As discussed, one of the hardest things about saving seeds from biennial crops—at least in a cold climate—is getting the crop through winter. This is worth discussing from a food storage aspect as well. I remember a city-dwelling aunt, upon seeing a picture of my onions curing on a rack, asking, "What can you possibly do with all of those onions?" Now this aunt is an amazing cook, so I replied, "Well, there are maybe 150 onions there—don't you use at least three or four onions a week?" "Of course, but won't they go bad before you can use them all?"

This, of course, is a modern view of the situation. After all, when we need onions—or other produce, for that matter—we go to the grocery store (or better yet, the farmers' market). It wasn't too long ago, however, that all winter, people went to get produce from their root cellar.

While we will, I believe, do the topic some justice here, for a detailed discussion of the root cellar, I highly recommend Mike and Nancy Bubel's 1979 Classic *Root Cellaring: Natural Cold Storage of Fruits and Vegetables* (Storey Publishing).

For the classic root cellar, think of an old farmhouse with a field stone foundation surrounding a cellar with a dirt floor. The cellar is cool and damp all year but (ideally) doesn't go below freezing in the winter. *That* is a *cellar* for storing fruits and veggies. What most of us have—a poured concrete foundation and a concrete floor, with a furnace and a water heater, and perhaps our out-of-season camping and sporting gear—that's not a cellar, it's a *basement*. If that's what you have, no matter. It's what we have, too. There are a number of strategies for getting what you need.

First of all, if you live in an area too warm to have a nice, cold root cellar, you're in luck! You probably don't need one. Many of the biennials will do just fine right out in your garden—both for eating and seed saving. Carrots, kale, leeks, parsnip will all be quite happy. Just give them a nice mulch of leaves or straw before a hard freeze and you can dig them all winter. Maybe put some mouse traps in the garden, too. There is nothing like pulling up a carrot by the crown to find what was supposed to be below is already eaten. Mice have good taste.

Now, some of us have garden soil that will be so frozen as to resemble concrete. What we need to create are cool, moist conditions somewhere between 32 and 40 degrees. If you only have a small amount of seed, a refrigerator can work reasonably well. It is certainly the right temperature. The problem is that is typically too dry, even in the crisper. I've had success with storing carrots and beets in plastic bags in the fridge, but again, space is limited.

If you are really motivated for some passive cold storage (passive meaning you aren't using electricity to power a refrigerator compressor), you can corner off a section of your basement. This is what we did in the northeast corner of our house. We placed studs floor to ceiling to corner off a section that included one high window and the bulkhead (the bulkhead is how you get out of a dug basement to the outside—think the entrance to Dorothy's storm cellar back in Kansas). We put insulation on the inside of the studs and on the ceiling, leaving the concrete walls and floors bare. I built an insulated door between the new "cellar" and our basement. I put weather seals around it, basically making it an exterior door. I have heard that some people rent a concrete saw to cut out a section of the floor to reveal the gravel below. Not being *quite* that ambitious, we left the floor as is.

We've had very good luck with the root cellar this way. We leave the bulkhead open on cool fall nights to get the temperature down, and leave it closed all winter so it doesn't freeze (this usually works). It is sufficiently cool and damp enough to store potatoes (the start to sprout in early April, so we put what's left in the fridge by late March). The air is a bit too dry to accommodate carrots, beets, and parsnips. In the classic root cellar, these are often placed in buckets of sand, but this becomes much too dry in our root

KEEPING IT SIMPLE

1. A root cellar is a place that is cool and moist to keep potatoes, carrots, cabbage, parsnips, beets, and other winter roots.
2. Old sandy cellars with stone walls and dirt floors work best, but accommodations can be made to a modern basement to make it more suitable.
3. For small quantities, a refrigerator can work well, but can be too dry. Store veggies in plastic bags in the crisper.
4. The cool (50 degrees) and dryish modern basement is the perfect place for onions, squash, sweet potatoes, and garlic. Make sure they are well cured.

cellar. We've solved that problem by storing these veggies in plastic bins from the hardware store—no sand needed. I know, *plastic!* How unromantic. Alas, sometimes we need to be practical, and were it not for those plastic bins, I might be running another whole fridge. On the balance, I see that as a good trade-off, and the bins have lasted for several years. The system has been sound enough to store everything described above, plus cabbages (for eating—I have not yet tried keeping the root on for a seed crop) and Jerusalem artichokes, among others. We also store leeks in buckets of garden soil (see the section on onion and leek storage), though it can be a bit dry for their tastes. We've not had a problem as long as, maybe once a month, we put some water in the soil around them.

The good news for those of us who have this more typical modern basement that tends to be a little drier and run about 50 degrees: this is the *perfect* place to store another group of crops. Onions, sweet potatoes, winter squash, pumpkins, and garlic will love this warm (by winter vegetable standards), drier environment. That is, assuming they are properly cured. Setting squash out in the sun for their rinds to harden is a must if you don't want to be carrying squishy squash out of your root cellar in the middle of the winter to congeal atop your frozen compost pile.

C. Threshing and Winnowing

When I first started saving dry beans (for food and seed), I would pull the pods off the plant one by one. We'd set them in a big pile until great-grandma's visit every October. She and my youngest daughter would sit together for hours and shell each bean by hand. The seed was perfectly clean and beautiful. However, as we scaled up, this started becoming impractical. The first year that I figured out how to thresh our bean seed, I was happy to report to great-grandma that her labors were at an end! I did not need her to painstakingly pull each bean from its pod. I explained with pride my technique for threshing and winnowing. To my shock, she looked appalled, and responded, "Oh, the curses of technology!" Scratching my head, I was tempted to point out that this technology was at least as old as the Egyptian pyramids—probably older. On the brink of this reply, I finally realized she simply liked sitting by our fire in the evening, her ancient hands sharing the annual ritual with my four-year-old's tiny fingers. Together, they blessed every seed as it came out of the pod.

As precious as these moments were, threshing has not only been a much more practical approach but has been equally fun—when not injurious. Don't worry, I shall explain!

For small crops of small-seeded things like lettuce, cilantro, and onions, hand threshing is the way to go. Simply hold the seed stock over a large bowl and clap it between your hands. Rub vigorously like you are trying to get warm. If you have a good dry seed head with lots of nice seed in it, you will see those seeds start to rain down into the bowl, while bits of chaff (pieces of broken leaves and stem) flurry about like snow. This is best to do outside, as it can make a bit of a mess. Once you have enough of the seed liberated, the next step is winnowing. Swirl the contents of the bowl like a miner panning for gold. While doing this, gently blow the chaff (which will have floated to the top) away, leaving the nice, heavy seed at the bottom. You will see some seed fly away, but remember, those are likely duds that won't germinate anyway.

For larger seeds like peas, beans, and grains, winnowing with a flail is the way to go. This is where the fun begins, but also the possibility for injury, so be careful!

Threshing with a flail is best done on a dry, sunny day. Get a large tarp that can handle a little beating. I like canvas painter's tarps that are available at many hardware and paint stores. The most important thing is that it can stand up to being whacked with a stick without getting holes. Lay the tarp out on dry, level ground. Place your dried plants on the tarp in heaps. Then very carefully, start to beat them with the flail.

What to use as a flail? The classic flail would be two sticks tied (securely) together with a rope. My most effective flail consists of two pieces of one-inch dowel. One is about two-and-a-half feet long, the other about 18 inches. Holes are drilled into one end of each, and they are connected by a piece of climbing rope. However you choose to do this, make sure the "flail" end is securely attached and can't go flying. For the kids—who will absolutely want to help—we use whiffle bats.

To hand thresh, place items to be threshed in a large container. For bean pods like this, a large bowl suffices, but dried seed heads from lettuce, kale, and the like may need a large plastic storage bin.

Rub the pods vigorously between your hands. Leather gloves can sometimes be useful.

Make sure it is throughly threshed.

A few suggestions for safety: 1) don't do this in pairs; 2) if you do it in pairs, don't stand across from each other; 3) don't let the kids use the big dowel rod flail until they are older; 4) the flail bounces and can come back at you; 5) you don't actually have to swing that hard. (OK, thanks for taking the trip down safety lane with me—it's just hard to put the dad in me aside!)

At this point, you just beat the dried plants with the flail until the pile is greatly reduced in size and there are oodles and oodles of nice, dry seeds at the bottom of the pile. You'll want to fluff it up a few times to make sure that you are getting at it all.

Once the seed is well loosened (and you have taken out all of your frustration, whichever happens second), lift up the pile of threshings that are over your seed. If you have chickens, they will *love* going through this to find everything you missed! Fold the tarp in half and then in quarters and lift it up so you have a sack of sorts. A partner helps to do this gracefully without spilling all the seed. Pour the seed into a five-gallon bucket or similar container. You then have to winnow it!

As with hand threshing, winnowing simply involves blowing away the light chaff to leave the heavy seed behind. At this scale, however, you can't really do it with your own breath. Some folks say to pour the seed from one bucket to the other on a windy day, and let the chaff blow away. I find this difficult as I have to wait for the right day, and the wind is unreliable. Too strong a breeze can blow my crop away! I have heard some folks have luck with using a fan to blow over the pile on the tarp as they sort out the heavier bits and stems. My favorite way is to reverse the hose on our shop vacuum, so that the air is blowing out. This make a nice, consistent, directional airflow that I can direct into the bucket to blow the chaff away. If the good seed gets so agitated it starts to come out, I just back off a bit and all is well. I also find that this

Winnow. Blow the chaff out of the bowl. You can use a fan or a canister vacuum on "blow", but for a small sample like this, the "birthday candle" method is usually sufficient. You can see this will need to be rethreshed a little.

KEEPING IT SIMPLE

To thresh and winnow plants (that is, separate the seed from the stems and leaves):
1. Dry plants well.
2. Smash them with your hands (small crops of small seeds) or a flail (larger crops, larger seeds).
3. Be careful!
4. Blow away the chaff with your breath, wind, a fan, or a vacuum in reverse.

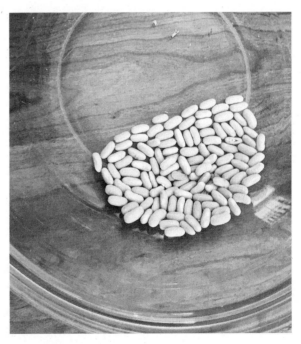

Clean seed!

works better in a plastic tote than in a five-gallon bucket, as you get a bit more surface area to work with.

For a seed crop, you are done at this point. For a food crop, you'll want to do one more step right before cooking. Put the beans (or whatever) into a pot and fill with water so there is an inch or two of space above. This will float off the last bits of chaff. Don't do this before storage, as that moisture, as we have discussed, is the enemy of longevity in storage.

D. Space-Saving Strategies

One of the biggest barriers many home gardeners have is space. Even if we have the pleasure of a garden with room to stretch our feet (and our rows), it's still nice to fill that space with—by and large—things to eat! Happily, there are a number of techniques we can use to make the most of our finite space.

1. Only grow a seed crop every few years. Most seeds will last for several years, so you don't need to make room in your garden for every seed every year. See the sidebar on Curing Seed, Seed Storage, and Longevity for more.

2. Grow seeds where the food crop is also the seed crop. We eat the seeds of dry beans, sunflower seeds, naked seeded pumpkin (pepita), and grains (wheat and barley), to name a few. Your only challenge to having a seed crop here is diverting your appetite!

3. Grow seeds from plants where you get both a food crop and a seed crop. Winter squash and pumpkins are good examples here. You typically compost the seed, so you may as well set some aside. Other plants like kale, lettuce, and parsley don't take offense at having some of the greens harvested in the juvenile stage. As noted in the section on parsley, I eat my parsley all winter and rely on its rich tap root to push up healthy foliage and a seed stalk come spring.

4. Grow seed plants thickly and thin for food as they grow. This is an excellent technique for greens, including kale and lettuce. The sexually mature plant needs space; the juvenile food crop not so much. Plant kale every twelve inches, eat every other one, and you end up with nice two-foot spacing for your seed crop.

Some ways *not* to save space: I don't recommend using puny, off-types not fit for eating. Sadly, I say this from experience. In addition to my disaster with using small, pencil-sized leeks for seed (see sidebar About Experimentation), I have also tried to use the first lettuce to *bolt* as my seed crop (*bolting* is when the plant effectively goes through puberty and sends up a seed stalk). After all, you can't eat it then—tastes all bitter, right? Well, when you save lettuce that bolts before it's time, guess what its babies do, too. Yep—you guessed it. They win the award for first to bolt, also. You, no doubt, could see that coming. Me? I had to make the mistake to learn it the hard way: for many of our plants, it's the very plant we want most to eat that we want to use as the parent for future generations.

E. A Drying House

Nothing is more unkind to seeds drying down in the gentle late summer sun than a week of hard rain. It is gut-wrenching to watch a pristine stand of almost-dry seeds turn into a soggy, mildewed, half-sprouting mess. One reason this is a particular challenge to seed savers is that we are waiting for most of our crops to get to that 11–13% moisture content. If it rains on our green beans or lettuce for eating, so be it! (Lettuce is simply in heaven.) If it rains hard on green bean or lettuce seed that is almost dried down—forget it! Thankfully there is a solution—the drying house!

The concept of a drying house takes advantage of the fact that most seeds do not resent being pulled from their roots before they are fully dried down for storage. Dry beans are a good example. As long as the seeds are plumped up, the pod walls have thinned, and they are the color they are supposed to be (black, red, etc.) they no longer really need those roots. By all means, leave them in the field as long as the forecast is good. But if several days of rain are predicted, cut them at their roots and put them up for drying. I have friends who feel

KEEPING IT SIMPLE

1. You can harvest most plants—stems and all—when the seed is fully formed and starting to dry down. Doing so can protect them from late summer rain that can ruin a crop.

2. Cure them by hanging them upside down in a place sheltered from rain and rodents. A screened-in porch works well.

strongly that pulling the plant up so as to keep the root attached (even with a little soil) is a good way to get all the last little bits of nourishment into the seeds as they dry. I find this approach leads to bits of soil and sand in my seed, so I cut the root off at the ground. Try both and see what works for you.

After you cut or pull the crop (leave the leaves on, at least—they provide surface area for dissipating moisture), they should be bundled for drying. This is a bit different for each crop (see separate sections). Ideally, the best place to hang them for drying is under cover, has good air circulation, and is relatively inaccessible to squirrels and other pests. Some crops will drop their seeds all over the floor. Lettuce and cilantro/coriander are notorious, here. Kale and other cabbage family members also. To address this, once they are dry—but not quite brittle—put them upside down in a paper shopping bag and let them cure for another week or two.

We built a room like this on the back of our house. It is 16 feet square, covered with a roof, and has screened-in sides to exclude ro-

Here we find garlic, rosemary, and beans all sharing a fall day in our drying house.

dents and beams for hanging the drying plants. The primary challenge is that my wife seems to think it is also a good place for tables, chairs, and late-summer dinner parties with our friends. Not only has she taken over my seed drying house with porch furniture, but she complains that the veggies hang so low as to bump into our guest's heads.

Even if you have to share such a drying house with a spouse with different plans, it is well worth it for nice, dry, clean seed. If you don't have access to such a place, there are definitely other options. Barns can be good, though rodents can be a problem. Hanging things inside is an option if you don't have much to dry. Even hanging plants upside down uncovered on a garden fence can provide some protection from rain by promoting air circulation and keeping wet seeds from lying directly on the soil.

PART VIII

Final Recommendations:
Try it!

As stated at the beginning, I have attempted to put enough information in this book to give you a good start, without saving so much as to be overwhelming. That said, you cannot learn to save seed by reading this or any other book—you have to try it. So go for it! Hopefully, I have shared enough that you won't repeat my mistakes. But you will make your own. After which, you will be much more knowledgeable than me, as I may have not made those mistakes yet. Though I hope I have plenty of time left to make them!

Wishing you sweet things in all of your gardening endeavors.

Index

A

acorn squash, 39
apples, 12–13, 22
artichokes, Jerusalem, 14
availability, 4

B

beans
    anatomy of, 20
    characteristics chart, 31
    and cross prevention, 26
    drying, 77
    open-pollinated vs.
        hybrid, 18
    pole beans, 33
    pollination of, 22
    propagation of, 31–33, 38
    True Red Cranberry Pole
        Bean, 7–8
bees, 22
beets, 23
biennials
    defined, 11
    easy, 53, 60
    propagation of, 45–52
    separating between years,
        28
    summary, 60
    and winter storage, 70–72
Big Max pumpkins, 40

blueberries, 22
bolting, 77
Bonsall, Will, 20, 43
Brandywine tomatoes, 17, 36
Brassica juncea, 59
Brassica napobrassica, 59
Brassica napus, 58
Brassica oleracea, 58
Brassica rapa, 59
broader horizons, 6–7
broccoli, 22, 58, 61
brussels sprouts, 58
Bubel, Mike and Nancy, 70
buttercup squash, 40
butternut squash, 40, 41

C

cabbage
    anatomy of, 20
    characteristics chart, 59
    pollination of, 22
    propagation of, 59–61
    summary, 60
caging, 29–30
canola, 58
carrots
    characteristics chart, 56
    and cross prevention, 28
    pollination of, 22
    propagation of, 56–57

and Queen Anne's lace, 30
    summary, 60
cauliflower, 58
cayenne peppers, 38
cellars, 70–72
chaff, 34
chard, 23
cheese pumpkins, 40
Cinderella pumpkins, 40
Clear Dawn onions, 17
collards, 58
Copra onions, 17
corn
    anatomy of, 20
    characteristics chart, 54
    open-pollinated vs. hybrid,
        18
    pollination of, 23
    propagation of, 53–56
    summary, 60
crossing
    outside your garden, 30
    prevention of. *see* cross
        prevention
    unintended, 28–29
cross prevention
    and biennials, 28
    caging, 29–30
    cross-resistant vegetables,
        25

hand pollination, 26
and separation between
    years, 28–29
and separation by space,
    26–27
and separation by time,
    27–29, 55
summary, 27
unintended, 27
cross-resistant vegetables, 25
cucumbers, 63–64
Cucurbita maxima, 40
Cucurbita moschata, 40, 41, 52
Cucurbita pepo, 39
curing, 67–68, 77
cuttings, 13

D
delicatas squash, 39
disease, 15
drying, 67–68
drying house, 77–79

E
evolution of your garden, 7–9
experimentation, 8

F
F1 hybrid, 18
feral plants, 30
fermentation, 36–37, 38
first filial hybrids, 18
flies, 22
flowers
    female and male parts, 36, 41
    perfect, 20, 21–22, 25
    and pollination, 32, 35–36,
        41–43
    and seed production, 13, 16

freezing, 68, 69
frugality, 5
fruit trees
    anatomy of, 20
    vegetative propagation,
        12–13
fungal disease, 15

G
Garden Seed Inventory, 4
garlic, 14, 15, 16, 71, 72
genetics. *see also* crossing
    of corn, 54
    inbreeding vs. outbreeding,
        24–25
    of peppers, 38
    and pollination, 13–14
germination test, 69
Gilfeather rutabagas, 59
grafting, 13, 15

H
hand pollination, 26, 41
harvesting, 77–78
herbs, 14
honeybees, 22
Howden pumpkins, 39
hubbard squash, 40
hybrids
    F1, 18
    first filial, 18
    introduction to, 17

I
inbreeding
    of corn, 54
    described, 25
    and perfect flowers, 31–38
    summary, 38

inbreeding depression, 46,
    53
insect pollination, 22–23

J
Jerusalem artichokes, 14

K
kabochas squash, 40
kale
    characteristics chart, 51
    pollination of, 22
    propagation of, 50–51
    quantity of seed, 4
    Siberian, 58, 60
    true, 58, 60
kohlrabi, 58

L
labeling, 69
larval pollinators, 30
leeks
    characteristics chart, 46
    pollination of, 22
    propagation of, 46, 48–49
    and selection, 8
lettuce
    characteristics chart, 33
    pollination of, 22
    propagation of, 33–35, 38
longevity, 68, 69

M
Mallory, George, 4
melons, 64
mosquitoes, 22
moving parts, 39–52
muskmelons, 64
mustard, 59, 61

N

naming, 7
New England Pie pumpkins, 39

O

obligate outbreeders, 60–61
onions
    characteristics chart, 46
    cross prevention, 45
    open-pollinated vs. hybrid, 17
    pollination of, 22
    propagation of, 46, 47–49, 52
    storage of, 71, 72
    summary, 52
open-pollinated plants, 17, 18
outbreeding, 23, 24–25, 60–61

P

Painted Mountain corn, 55
parsley
    characteristics chart, 50
    pollination of, 22
    propagation of, 50
parsnips
    characteristics chart, 56
    propagation of, 58
    summary, 60
pears, 13, 22
peas
    anatomy of, 20
    characteristics chart, 31
    and cross prevention, 26
    pollination of, 22
    propagation of, 31–33, 38
peppers
    anatomy of, 20
    cayenne peppers, 38

characteristics chart, 37
    pollination of, 22
    propagation of, 38
perfect flowers
    beans, 31–33
    defined, 20
    and inbreeding, 31–38
    lettuce, 33–35
    peas, 31–33
    and self-pollination, 21–22, 25
ping test, 67
placenta, 20
poison parsnip, 58
pole beans, 33
pollen, 20
pollination
    defined, 24
    and genetics, 13–14
    by hand, 26, 41–43
    by insects, 22–23
    by larval pollinators, 30
    self, 21–22
    summary, 24
    by wind, 23–24
potatoes, 13–14, 15
potato-leaf tomatoes, 36
propagation. *see also specific plants*
    crossing. *see* crossing
    inbreeding vs. outbreeding, 24–25
    promiscuity vs. prudence, 25–30
    sexual, 16, 20
    vegetative, 11–16
Pruden's Purple tomatoes, 36
pumpkins, 27–28, 42, 44, 72. *see also* squash

purity, 23. *see also* cross prevention
Purple Cherokee tomatoes, 36

Q

Queen Anne's lace, 30, 56

R

rain, 33
rapeseed, 58
reasons to save seed, 4–9
Root Cellaring (Bubel), 70
root cellars, 70–72
rosemary, 15–16
Russian tomatoes, 7
rutabagas, 59, 61

S

scapes, 15
Scatterseed Project, 20
scion wood, 15
seed garlic, 16
seed potatoes, 16
Seed Savers Exchange, 4
selection, 7, 8
self-pollination, 21–22
Seminole pumpkins, 40
separation between years, 28–29
separation by space, 26–27
separation by time, 27–29, 55
sexual propagation
    anatomy, 20
    introduction to, 16
    methods of, 21–24
    pollination methods, 21–24
    summary, 16
sharing, 6, 55

Siberian kale, 58, 60

small scale, 2–3

space saving, 76–77

spacing, 41

spaghetti squash, 39

sperm, 20

spinach

    anatomy of, 20

    characteristics chart, 44

    propagation of, 44–45, 52

    summary, 52

squash

    anatomy of, 20

    characteristics chart, 40

    and cross prevention, 26, 27

    flowers of, 19

    hand pollination of, 41–43

    pollination of, 22

    propagation of, 39–44, 52

    storage of, 71, 72

    summary, 52

stabilization, 17

storage, 15, 68, 70–72

strawberries, 12

summer squash, 39

sunflowers, 64–65

sunflowers, 19

Sungold tomatoes, 17

sweet potatoes, 14, 71, 72

T

threshing, 72–74, 75

tillers, 34

tomatoes

    anatomy of, 20

    characteristics chart, 35

    and cross prevention, 26

    fermentation of seeds,

        36–37, 38

    open-pollinated vs. hybrid,

        17

    pollination of, 22, 35–36

    potato-leaf varieties, 36

    propagation of, 35–37

    Russian, 7

    as volunteers, 19

    Zurovchak, 7

True Red Cranberry Pole

    Bean, 7–8

true to type, 13

turnips, 59, 61

U

unintended crosses, 27, 28–29

V

variety

    as benefit of seed saving, 6

    defined, 17

open-pollinated vs. hybrid,

    17–18

vegetative propagation

    apples, 12–13

    challenges of, 14

    fruit trees, 12–13

    garlic, 14

    herbs, 14

    Jerusalem artichokes, 14

    potatoes, 13–14, 15

    summary, 16

    sweet potatoes, 14

volunteers, 19

W

wasps, 22

watermelons, 64

wild plants, 30

wind pollination, 23–24

winnowing, 73, 74–76

winter squash, 39, 72

woody herbs, 14

Y

Yellow Pear tomatoes, 36

Z

zucchini, 27, 39

Zurovchak tomatoes, 7, 26, 27

About the Author

JIM ULAGER is a home gardener and seed saver who has traveled, studied, and spoken on seed saving for the small-scale gardener. Jim speaks at the Common Ground Fair, garden clubs, and seed saving organizations, and also produces fruit, vegetables, tree products, chicken, pork, grain, and seeds on his 4-acre Vermont homestead with his wife and 3 children.

ABOUT NEW SOCIETY PUBLISHERS

New Society Publishers is an activist, solutions-oriented publisher focused on publishing books for a world of change. Our books offer tips, tools, and insights from leading experts in sustainable building, homesteading, climate change, environment, conscientious commerce, renewable energy, and more—positive solutions for troubled times.

We're proud to hold to the highest environmental and social standards of any publisher in North America. This is why some of our books might cost a little more. We think it's worth it!

- We print all our books in North America, never overseas
- All our books are printed on **100% post-consumer recycled paper**, processed chlorine-free, with low-VOC vegetable-based inks (since 2002)
- Our corporate structure is an innovative employee shareholder agreement, so we're one-third employee-owned (since 2015)
- We're carbon-neutral (since 2006)
- We're certified as a B Corporation (since 2016)

At New Society Publishers, we care deeply about *what* we publish—but also about *how* we do business.

Download our catalog at https://newsociety.com/Our-Catalog or for a printed copy please email info@newsocietypub.com or call 1-800-567-6772 ext 111.

New Society Publishers
ENVIRONMENTAL BENEFITS STATEMENT

For every 5,000 books printed, New Society saves the following resources:[1]

13	Trees
1,213	Pounds of Solid Waste
1,335	Gallons of Water
1,741	Kilowatt Hours of Electricity
2,205	Pounds of Greenhouse Gases
9	Pounds of HAPs, VOCs, and AOX Combined
3	Cubic Yards of Landfill Space

[1] Environmental benefits are calculated based on research done by the Environmental Defense Fund and other members of the Paper Task Force who study the environmental impacts of the paper industry.